CLASSROOM STRATEGIES FOR SECONDARY READING

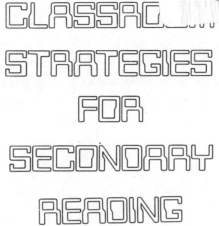

Second Edition

Edited by W. John Harker

University of Victoria

INTERNATIONAL READING ASSOCIATION
800 Barksdale Road, Box 8139
Newark, Delaware 19714

INTERNATIONAL READING ASSOCIATION

Copyright 1985 by the
International Reading Association, Inc.

Library of Congress Cataloging in Publication Data
Main entry under title:

Classroom strategies for secondary reading.

Includes bibliographies.
1. Reading (Secondary education)—Addresses, essays, lectures. 2. Reading comprehension—Addresses, essays, lectures. 3. Study, Method of—Addresses, essays, lectures. 4. Instructional systems—Planning—Addresses, essays, lectures. I. Harker, W. John.
LB1632.C555   1985   428.4'0712   84-28939
ISBN 0-87207-605-9

CONTENTS

Foreword *v*

Introduction *vi*

FOREWORD

"My kids can't read their textbooks!" "But, every teacher is a teacher of reading!" Both of those positions are a result of the dominant role the textbook plays in the secondary schools. Many teachers place the responsibility for learning on the textbook, or on the students' inability to learn from that textbook.

The textbook is only a tool and should be used by, not in place of, the teacher. However, when that textbook is used, the teacher should have at hand strategies that have been shown to improve students' comprehension.

This second edition of *Classroom Strategies for Secondary Reading* is aimed at providing content area teachers with some of those strategies.

Knowing *what* these strategies are is very important but knowing *why* we use them is essential. Therefore, this monograph will be very useful as a tool for content area teachers who do not have easy access to the *Journal of Reading* and wish to supplement the *why* provided to them by a reading consultant at the building, school, or college level.

Judie Thelen
Frostburg (MD) State College

INTRODUCTION

It is encouraging that this second edition of *Classroom Strategies for Secondary Reading* has been made possible by the success of the first edition. The intent of the first edition was to meet the practical requirements of secondary content area teachers who wanted to teach reading and study skills as a means of furthering their students' learning of content, but who were unsure where to begin or what to do. From the response to the first edition it is clear this focus met the needs of many teachers. It is equally clear these needs persist for other teachers. Therefore, this second edition.

This book is aimed at providing the practising or prospective content area teacher with a sequence of steps through which classroom reading programs in the content areas can be developed. In Section 1 teachers are given suggestions for assessing the status of their students' reading and study skills development. However, content area teachers often realize the reading and study skills difficulties of their students and they want to know more than the fact that there is a problem; they want to know what to do about it. But assessment, when it is specifically focused on the particular demands of learning in the different content areas, is the first step toward answering the question of what to do, and therefore it is the place to start. From the information assessment reveals, teachers then can proceed to the suggestions given in Section 2 to determine general instructional strategies, which will focus on content area instructional objectives (what teachers want students to learn about their subject), and on the development of students' ability to exercise the reading and study skills they will find necessary to achieve these objectives. In Section 3, after determining instructional strategies, teachers are shown either how to select instructional materials appropriate to both content area learning objectives and the level of students' skills development or, if faced with the more common situation of mandated instructional materials where selection is not possible, how to evaluate these materials so that their strengths can be built upon and their weaknesses avoided. Having determined the materials, teachers can plan specific skills instruction aimed at placing students in the centre of the learning process as they integrate skills acquisition with content learning. Section 4 provides guidance for this planning. Finally, in Section 5, the general nature of reading programs is considered in recognition that no matter how careful the planning and implementation of each of the above steps, the entirety of a program will exceed the sum of its parts and in the final analysis be the measure of its success.

How this book will be used will vary with the needs and expectations of the user. Ideally, it will form the basis for planning reading programs in content area classrooms either by individual teachers or by groups of teachers interested in developing school or districtwide programs based on reading and study skill instruction in each content area classroom. In either case, the sequence of steps outlined above should help. But other teachers may wish to consult individual sections of the book or specific articles within each section for guidance in planning specific aspects of reading programs or for additional information to augment existing programs. The organization of the book permits and encourages this kind of selective use as well.

The appearance of a second edition raises a question. Have the needs of teachers and the directions given to them in the professional literature changed in the years since the first edition appeared? It is clear that teachers' perceptions of their needs have grown as the conventional wisdom of contemporary education has given more and more recognition to the integration of reading and study skill instruction with content area instruction. Yet it is equally clear that teachers, especially content area teachers, while aware of this stress on integration, have become even more confused and frustrated due to their continuing lack of adequate preservice education in secondary reading.

So the need persists. But what about the response to this need in the professional literature? With the growing recognition of the value of integrated skills and content instruction, there has at the same time developed a changing emphasis on the role of the teacher and the place of the student in the instructional process. In the first instance, reading and study skill teaching has become increasingly teacher directed. No longer is a reliance on standardized tests and "special" instructional materials for content area reading as apparent as it once was. More and more, the expertise of the content area teacher is being credited for determining which reading and study skills should be taught, through which materials they should be taught, and how they should be measured. This places more responsibility on the teacher and gives the teacher greater flexibility in determining the specific nature and manner of instruction. With this emphasis on teacher direction there has emerged a complementary emphasis on student centered instruction. No longer is the teacher's role perceived to be one of applying a variety of pedagogical Band-Aids often in the form of colourful prepackaged materials and electronic gadgetry. In contrast, the centrality of the student in the learning process is gaining increased recognition. The teacher is coming to be seen as the facilitator of students' learning, not as the director. The teacher is being recognized as the one person who, by clarifying the process of learning and rationalizing it, enables students to experience success on their own terms using reading material which gains significance for them. In this way, more and more recognition is being given to teaching students how to learn from content area material rather than remaining preoccupied with the nature and manipulation of this material for its own sake.

These are all exciting and progressive developments to which teachers will respond if given the chance. Hopefully, this short book will aid in this response by providing some practical guidance which is based on a sound theory of instruction.

WJH

Section One

ASSESSMENT

The first step in planning content area reading instruction is to assess students' preparedness to comprehend the material they will be expected to read. Here the term "readiness" is useful to conceptualize the specific intent and method of this assessment. Although teachers normally hear "readiness" used to refer to primary children's preparedness to undertake beginning reading instruction, the concept the term represents — readiness to undertake new learning — is equally appropriate to the secondary grades. At this level, it means that the teacher will assess whether the students are "ready" to read the new materials which will confront them in the content area classroom. The nature and extent of this readiness will vary among individual students, different grade levels and different classes within the same grade level, specific content areas, and particular instructional situations. But the general objective will be the same — to determine the extent to which students possess the reading and study skills they require for successful reading in particular learning situations in particular content areas.

While various methods are often suggested to teachers for determining these skills, the most valid one is for teachers to place themselves in the "conceptual shoes" of their students. This involves paying due regard to such variables as students' previous learning in the content area concerned, the level of independence in learning to be expected of them, and their likely motivation. Once this cognitive stance is assumed, teachers can simulate in their own minds the learning process to be required of their students during content area reading. Through this process of conceptually "walking through" the learning task of the students from the students' perspective, teachers can gain a clearer understanding of the kinds of skills and abilities their students will need in order to achieve the levels of comprehension required for successful content area learning.

It is on the basis of this determination of skills that teachers can undertake an assessment of students' readiness for content area learning. The skills determined will be the skills assessed. And on the basis of this assessment teachers will gain a clearer picture of which skills need to be taught, and which skills students already possess. In this way, functionality, precision, and economy of instruction are all gained from only a relatively small amount of time spent on assessment.

In this section, two articles provide direction for the kind of assessment teachers can undertake and adapt to the particular demands of their own content areas and teaching situations. In the first, Hansell describes four general methods by which teachers may informally assess their students' readiness for learning. A further and more recent method is supplied by Irwin and Mitchell in the second article. Here they outline a procedure for determining students' level of understanding by asking them to retell what they have read. In both of these articles, a move away from standardized testing is apparent. In both cases, teachers are given ways of assessing their students' reading and study skill status free from what has come to be recognized as a major limitation of standardized tests—their failure to provide valid and reliable measures of the specific skills students required for content area reading. As an alternative, teachers are shown how to develop tests of their own, tests which may lack the statistical rigor of standardized tests, but provide more independence and precision in determining just which reading and study skills students need to be taught. In this way, teachers should realize the truth of what has been said of them for many years—that they are the real experts in content area reading instruction, since they are in the best position to determine the specific skills needs of their students.

- *What are the strengths and weaknesses of each method outlined?*
- *How might these methods be combined to provide a comprehensive assessment of students' readiness for learning?*

FOUR METHODS OF DIAGNOSIS FOR CONTENT AREA READING

T. Stevenson Hansell
Wright State University

If you are a content area teacher, your key to selecting reachable short term goals for a unit is to diagnose where your students already stand in relation to the material: Do they already know some of the basic concepts? Can they handle the vocabulary they will be reading or must you teach it? Are their overall reading skills up to the level of the material you plan to use? Every content area puts different demands on students. You can often, through instruction, help them comprehend the reading material better, but to provide just the right instruction, you must know how to diagnose your students' weak spots.

Simons (1971) discussed seven approaches to measuring comprehension. I will discuss the four that a content area teacher could use most readily: the readability approach, the skills perspective, the introspective report, and the models approach.

Readability Approach

The readability approach is quick and easy, although it diagnoses the textbook rather than the student. Using a readability formula or scale, you calculate an average grade level for the text. Students who can read at that level should be able to comprehend the material. (Any reading teacher in your school can provide a formula and show you how to apply it, or you can look up Fry, 1968 or SMOG, McLaughlin, 1969).

The danger of the readability approach is twofold. First, not all students in a class read at the same level or in the same manner—each brings different background knowledge and skills to reading. Thus a readability for-

Adapted from *Journal of Reading*, May 1981, *24*, 696-700.

mula may suggest that a text is at the seventh grade level, but not every student in an eighth grade class is necessarily able to read it with comfort. Many need instruction to help them cope with the text.

Second, the ease with which texts can be read does not correspond directly with their readability scores (Hansell, 1976). Formulas measure only things that can be counted, such as the number of words not on a list of common vocabulary (Dale-Chall), the number of syllables per unit of length (Fry & smog), and the number of words per sentence. They say nothing about the organization or clarity of a text. More importantly, they say nothing about the reader, nor the purpose for which the material is to be read (Hansell, 1974).

In sum, readability ratings are one way to estimate the relative difficulty of textbooks, but they are clearly not appropriate as the sole means of diagnosis.

Skills Approach

The skills approach to evaluating content reading ability is common — virtually every text on elementary, content, or secondary reading includes a list of skills students need, ranging from what Herber and Riley (1979) call the "simplest form" of list (vocabulary, comprehension, and reasoning) to composites that include every imaginable skill and subskill.

The skills perspective generates observational checklists (e.g., Barbe, Converse, & Converse, 1976), placement tests (coordinated with workbooks, basal kits, basal readers, taped programs), and a wide variety of teacher designed tests. However, guidelines provided by Burmeister (1978), Shepherd (1978), Strang (1964), and Thelen (1976) show how teachers can use their own textbooks to determine whether their students have the skills needed to read them. The teacher gives the students 20 to 35 questions about the book in general (e.g., its length and organization), its parts, its vocabulary, and word recognition skills that will be helpful (e.g., knowledge of suffixes), plus questions that assess students' general comprehension and speed during reading of a selected passage from that text.

The results show whether the students have grasped the overall structure of the material, whether they know key vocabulary items and can cope with the sorts of words they'll encounter, and whether they can comprehend a sample passage from the text and read it with a speed that indicates comprehension rather than word by word decoding. If students do poorly on any aspect of the inventory, you know which areas will require special instruction while students are using that book.

Burmeister (1978, p. 50) and Estes and Vaughan (1978, p. 78) suggest an inventory of just 15 questions over an excerpt from the material: five questions on details, five on main ideas, and five that require students to interpret and use information from the text. Shepherd (1978, p. 86) would add questions about sequence of events and drawing conclusions, to which Strang (1964, p. 129) would add organization of details and following directions.

To make the inventory relevant, you prepare it over a passage of 1,500 to 3,000 words (Burmeister, 1978, p. 49) from the text you intend to use. You introduce this passage to your class just as you normally introduce a reading activity, pointing out (but in this case not defining) vocabulary terms, and eliciting questions from each student about the passage. Each student then reads the assignment, records the time it required and then completes the inventory.

Thelen (1976) suggests using a similar approach after the students have previewed the text as a whole. As an introductory task, each student spends three minutes discovering as much as possible about the text, then answers questions about the most important points of the text, the reason the book was written, and its organizational parts, as well as its size, weight, color, title, and author. This orientation helps students see the text as a whole rather than as separate pieces.

These informal content reading inventories should, of course, measure only the skills and information the students will actually use with your planned content, procedures, and materials.

If you are developing your inventory with the help of a list of reading skills, you may wish to keep in mind some of Simons' criticisms (1971, p. 343) of the skills approach to evaluating comprehension. He notes that the lists often contain global and poorly defined terms; there is confusion about what can be called reading comprehension; there is no distinction between the product of comprehension (e.g., outlining) and the underlying processes (e.g., identifying main ideas and perceiving the organization of the passage, both of which are necessary for outlining).

Some specialists also feel that the skills approach leads to unnecessary fragmentation of instruction. Clearly, any student who can outline a passage can already identify main ideas, draw conclusions, make inferences, and perceive the organization of ideas in the passage, since all of these skills are used in outlining. For this student, teaching the subskills is unnecessary. However, if some students cannot outline a text, a close examination of the attempt may show which part of the task is difficult for them in relation to the material read.

Introspective Report

In contrast to the product-oriented skills perspective, the introspective approach focuses on what a student feels is easy or difficult about reading, and on each student's study habits. Strang (1964, p. 85) suggests that after students have read an assignment in class they should be asked questions such as: "What did you do to get the main idea? What did you do to remember the details? What did you do when you met a word you didn't know?" Each student answers the questions about a particular passage. Additionally, Shepherd (1978, p. 36) suggests asking "What do you think is necessary to improve your reading or to overcome your difficulties?"

While introspective questions may help a teacher gain insight about a student's reading, accurate responses are not guaranteed. As semanticists such as Johnson (1968) have said, the same process may be described in several ways; changing the description does not change the process. Introspective accounts are also retrospective; that is, a student is asked to describe the reading process only afterwards. Perhaps introspective statements are influenced by the fact that the passage has been completed.

While the problem of description in introspective approaches cannot be overcome, the problem of retrospection has been, Olshavsky's procedure (1976-1977) is to ask a student to stop after each independent clause and say aloud what s/he is thinking. This diagnosis is best done individually but can provide great insight into a student's ability to understand specific material.

The introspective report focuses on the process of understanding, whereas the skills perspective focuses on the products. At the same time, both deal with many of the same aspects of content reading, e.g., main ideas, details, and vocabulary. Both differ from the readability approach by their emphasis on content.

Models of Comprehension

The models perspective sees skills as interrelated and attempts to explain how the comprehension process is related to its products.

In a model based on linguistics, Goodman (1969) proposes that a reader's mistakes are clues to the reading process that produced them. The teacher examines each oral reading error (miscue) to see whether the correct word was nevertheless grammatically appropriate (suggesting that the reader was aware of the sentence structure but did not know the vocabulary item) and whether it fit the meaning of both the sentence and the passage. Sensible mistakes, particularly when the student self-corrects them, indicate that a student can probably cope with the material.

Hansell

Miscue analysis can certainly be used with content passages. However, since it must be given to students individually, it is impractical for large classes.

The cloze procedure (Taylor, 1953) is a group paper and pencil instrument. Every fifth word of a passage is deleted and each student completes the passage by filling in the empty spaces. To see what a student is able to do, we must examine cloze results for more than exact word replacement. If the student's answers fit with the words before the blank but not with the rest of the sentence, the student is probably reading word by word. Similarly, some substitutions make sense within the passage while others do not. Careful examination of cloze responses may be carried out with Goodman's categories for miscue analysis, but common sense often gives an idea of what a particular student did to arrive at an answer.

My own model of reading (Hansell, 1979) includes memory, purpose, and word identification. Memory directly influences the latter two, since it includes experiences, knowledge of language, a semantic store of related concepts, and a system for logical evaluation.

Implications from this model suggest several diagnostic approaches. First, a mature reader often establishes a purpose for reading content material and may deal with the same material in different ways, depending on the purpose. A teacher can evaluate students' ability to set purposes by having them preview a selection for three to five minutes. Each student then writes out either questions which s/he thinks are important to answer while reading (Robinson, 1961) or hypotheses about what specific information will be included in the passage. Alternatively, a teacher might ask students to list hypotheses in answer to a teacher question (Stauffer, 1979) or to select from a list of purposes those which are most appropriate for the passage and setting (Stauffer, 1975).

Equally important is a student's ability to achieve the purposes set. The measure of comprehension is then the student's ability to read to answer the questions or evaluate the hypotheses that had been formed before reading.

Since comprehension is also affected by the amount of experience a reader has had with the content being discussed, you may want to assess student experience. This can be done through questionnaires or by listening and observing. Questionnaires can include open ended questions (e.g., "What do you know about fertilizers?") or specific items related to the topic (e.g., "True or false: For tomatoes, use a 10-5-5 fertilizer").

Semantic background knowledge may be evaluated before reading by giving students a key concept and asking them to list every word they know which is related to it (Herber & Riley, 1979). Four or five minutes is sufficient for this.

Similarly, Estes and Vaughan (1978, p. 101) suggest a class discussion of key terms or phrases using the question "What does it mean to you when I say...." This type of discussion reveals terms for which students have concepts different from the teacher's or author's.

In practice, the skills approach and the models approach to diagnosis are very similar. Distinctions are made by a teacher's knowledge and purpose. You may choose to teach skills in isolation from content or as a part of learning the content. If you know a models approach, you will take care to design activities which check the process of student learning as well as the products.

In summary, informal evaluation of content reading ability discovers what a student can do in relation to your goals for a study unit. Diagnosis is an intermediate step which logically falls between establishing clear goals and planning actual classroom operations. Whether you elect to use the perspectives of readability, skills, introspection, or models of reading, the instruments you select should provide information in relation to the unit's goals.

References

Barbe, Walter, Jerome Converse, and Valerie Converse. *Reading Skills Checklist and Activities,* 7th level. West Nyack, N.Y.: Center for Applied Research in Education, Inc., 1976.

Burmeister, Lou E. *Reading Strategies for Middle and Secondary School Teachers,* 2nd ed. Reading, Mass.: Addison-Wesley Publishing Co., 1978.

Estes, Thomas H., and Joseph L. Vaughan, Jr. *Reading and Learning in the Content Classroom: Diagnostic and Instructional Strategies,* abridged edition. Boston, Mass.: Allyn and Bacon, Inc., 1978.

Fry, Edward A. "A Readability Formula that Saves Time." *Journal of Reading,* vol. 11 (April 1968), pp. 513-16.

Goodman, Kenneth S. "Analysis of Oral Reading Miscues: Applied Psycholinguistics." *Reading Research Quarterly,* vol. 5 (Fall 1969), pp. 9-30.

Hansell, T. Stevenson. "Readability, Syntactic Transformations, and Generative Semantics." *Journal of Reading,* vol. 19 (January 1976) pp. 307-10.

Hansell, T. Stevenson. "The Effects of Manipulation of Syntax and Vocabulary on Reading Comprehension." Doctoral dissertation, University of Virginia, Charlottesville, 1974.

Hansell, T. Stevenson. "The Reading Process." *The Wright Stater* (December 1979), pp. 3-8.

Herber, Harold, and James D. Riley. *Research in Reading in the Content Areas: A Fourth Report.* Syracuse, N.Y.: Syracuse University Reading and Language Arts Center, 1979.

Johnson, Alexander Bryant. *A Treatise on Language.* New York, N.Y.: Dover Publications, Inc. 1968.

McLaughlin, G. H. "SMOG Grading—A New Reliability Formula." *Journal of Reading,* vol. 12 (May 1969), pp. 639-46.

Olshavsky, Jill Edwards. "Reading as Problem Solving: An Investigation of Strategies." *Reading Research Quarterly,* vol. 12 (1976-1977), pp. 654-74.

Robinson, Francis P. *Effective Study: Revised Edition.* New York, N.Y.: Harper and Row Publishers, 1961.

Shepherd, David L. *Comprehensive High School Reading Methods,* 2nd ed. Columbus, Ohio: Charles E. Merrill, 1978.

Simons, Herbert D. "Comprehension: A New Perspective." *Reading Research Quarterly,* vol. 6 (Spring 1971), pp. 338-63.

Stauffer, Russell G. *Directing the Reading-Thinking Process.* New York, N.Y.: Harper and Row, 1975.

Stauffer, Russeil G. Personal communication, Sept., 1979.

Strang, Ruth. *Diagnostic Teaching of Reading.* New York, N.Y.: McGraw Hill Book Co., 1964.

Taylor, Wilson. "Cloze Procedure: A New Tool for Measuring Readability." *Journalism Quarterly,* vol. 30 (1953), pp. 415-33.

Thelen, Judith. *Improving Reading in Science.* Newark, Del.: International Reading Association, 1976.

- *How can the set of criteria given here for evaluating retellings be modified to suit reading material in different content areas?*
- *What cautions do the authors raise for using their checklist?*

A PROCEDURE FOR ASSESSING THE RICHNESS OF RETELLINGS

Pi A. Irwin
Lee Instruction Center
Tucson, Arizona

Judy Nichols Mitchell
University of Arizona

A reader's recall or retelling of what s/he has read has long been recognized as a way to gain insights concerning comprehension (Bartlett, 1932). The past decade has marked an acceleration in the use of retellings in research studies and for assessment purposes. Hence, interest in evaluating the quality of retellings in the most appropriate manner has increased.

This interest has centered on just what it is in a retelling that indicates high, average, or low reader comprehension. Clearly, retellings are as various as the readers making them. Stated simply, then, we asked two questions. What characteristics of a retelling distinguish different levels of understanding of the text? Which retellings are superior—those in which the reader restates the passage content in accurate, precise detail or those in which the reader makes in-depth generalizations about life as s/he summarizes the text content?

Current methods of evaluating retellings have not clarified this matter to any extent. Generally, these methods arbitrarily assign points to reflect the relative importance of various elements of the retelling, such as inclusion of character, plot, setting, major points, or manner of organization (Clark, 1982; Goodman & Burke, 1971; Smith, 1980).

In contrast, what appears to be needed are systems for evaluating retellings which incorporate the balance among aspects of the text and the effect of the whole.

Adapted from *Journal of Reading*, February 1983, *26*, 391-396.

To gain these latter advantages, we developed and tested a holistic approach for evaluating student retellings, as described below.

Point Systems

Let us begin by looking at the disadvantages of the usual point systems for evaluating oral retellings. First, point assignment systems do not capture the interrelationships of all the individual factors nor the individuality of a student's point of view. Points are assigned to some factors but not others. The factors are selected a priori. Often no provision is made for evaluating other aspects of a student's retelling, such as summary statements, interpretations, and generalizations from the text to the student's own experiences. Biases for and against some types of information may be introduced as part of the evaluation process, which seems counter to the notion of retelling as "free recall."

The following excerpts from oral retellings of two tenth graders well illustrate the dilemmas encountered in assessing retellings by assigning points to various aspects.

Reader one

In the passage what was discussed was the girl's feelings about the raincoat her mother had bought her. She wanted a yellow slicker, just wanted to be like everybody else. Instead, her mother wanted her to stand out with this pink raincoat, so she got really angry when her mother bought her a pink raincoat and throws the roses down the disposal which was quite funny.

Reader two

This is like basically a short story and it's about a girl who wants to be part of the crowd and she's having problems so like in a point of rebellion she throws all the roses she was going to arrange down the disposal as a way of getting back at her mother for buying her this pink raincoat. She's like the type of girl that wants to be part of the crowd, which is real important like, you know, she's probably like a freshman or something in high school, that's supposed to be something like really big. I was thinking how this type of story will really relate to like you know, lots of kids, you know, who are younger and all because it's like when you're going to school you have to conform, you know, you're the oddball and that's what no one wants to be. She thinks by wearing this raincoat she'll be an oddball...these kind of stories really, what they do is they take like an ordinary situation and make it into a story which a kid can read and feel like, oh, I'm glad that, you know, see how they solve their problems and maybe help themselves by going through the story.

The protocol of reader one includes statements about plot, characters, and setting. It further contains an evaluative statement. In contrast, the protocol of reader two shows all of these components but also extends beyond the text to incorporate interpretative and generalizing statements. Using current scoring systems, these retellings, while distinctively different, may be assigned the same score. The real difference in the richness of understanding shown may be masked by assigning points.

While concerns exist with regard to scoring retellings, comparison of the two retellings above indicates how useful they can be because of what they reveal about reader comprehension. As Smith (1980) has noted, retellings, at a minimum, tell us what the reader recalls. A retelling may also show us what the reader adds to or infers from the text. Finally, retellings indicate how the reader creates a text for his/her own understanding. Insights about these differing aspects of reading comprehension can be gained because students give retellings in their own language, emphasizing what they feel is of importance. In this way, retellings offer a perspective not available through other means of assessing comprehension, such as questioning or cloze procedures.

In evaluating 48 student retellings, we needed to differentiate among retellings with varying proportions of reader's recall, inferencing, and individuality of retelling style. Assigning points seemed inappropriate because we had too many types of text samples to assure consistency in rating via a point system. Further, we were concerned with evaluating the retellings in an integrated, holistic fashion, rather than evaluating only those aspects of a text which merited points according to a predetermined system and ignoring other retelling features. Finally, we wanted to acknowledge the uniqueness of the way in which each reader had "created" his/her own retelling.

Rating of 48 Oral Retelling Protocols

Rating level	Expository text	Narrative text
5	1	2
4	3	7
3	12	13
2	7	2
1	1	0
Total	24	24

Evaluating the Total Product

In our thinking, a retelling could be likened to a tapestry which, while composed of many different colored strands, can be properly viewed and appreciated only in its totality. Examination of any given section of tapestry yields only an accumulation of the components. Its richness — its essence — the very qualities which define it as a tapestry — must be experienced in terms of its total impression.

Likewise, each reader's retelling is unique—stamped with the reader's personality, reaction, understanding. To capture these qualities, retellings must be assessed as totalities.

A model for evaluating the essence or richness of readers' retellings is provided by holistic grading systems for students' written compositions (Cooper, 1977; Myers, 1980). Essentially, holistic grading is based on two premises: that the whole of any piece of writing is greater than the sum of its parts (punctuation, sentence structure, spelling, etc.) and that the total impression of a writing sample includes everything we know about writing.

Additionally, use of holistic grading has shown that teachers using the same criteria make similar judgments about the quality of students' writing. This appears to be the case even thought those same teachers differ among themselves about the individual factors involved in the total composing process. As Cooper (1977, p. 19) has noted:

> When raters are from similar backgrounds and when they are trained with a holistic scoring guide—either one they borrow or devise for themselves on the spot—they can achieve nearly perfect agreement in choosing the better of a pair of essays; and they can achieve scoring reliabilities in the high eighties and low nineties on their summed scores from multiple pieces of a student's writing.

We believe that the principles of holistic grading can be used to evaluate retellings by capturing the richness or essence of readers' comprehension. We also feel that retellings, like writing samples, are best viewed in their totality rather than in their isolated parts. Finally, we assume that teachers who use the same criteria for evaluating retellings will make similar judgments.

To judge retellings on a holistic basis, we developed a set of criteria which include many features contained in other retelling scoring schemes. However, these criteria were not to be used to assign points but rather to identify characteristics of five distinct levels of richness. The criteria are described in Figure 1, Judging Richness of Retellings. Additionally, from the criteria we developed a Checklist for Judging Richness of Retellings (Figure 2) as a means of categorizing the principal qualities of each level of richness in comparison with all other levels.

We then used our system to evaluate oral retellings of 24 tenth grade students. Each student had read both a short story and an expository passage. In all, there were 12 short stories and 12 expository passages, so that each passage was read by 2 students. Results of our 48 ratings appear in the Table.

Figure 1
Judging Richness of Retellings

Level	Criteria for establishing level
5	Student generalizes beyond text; includes thesis (summarizing statement), all major points, and appropriate supporting details; includes relevant supplementations; shows high degree of coherence, completeness, comprehensibility.
4	Student includes thesis (summarizing statement), all major points, and appropriate supporting details; includes relevant supplementations; shows high degree of coherence, completeness, comprehensibility.
3	Student relates major ideas; includes appropriate supporting details and relevant supplementations; shows adequate coherence, completeness, comprehensibility.
2	Student relates a few major ideas and some supporting details; includes irrelevant supplementations; shows some degree of coherence, some completeness; the whole is somewhat comprehensible.
1	Student relates details only; irrelevant supplementations or none; low degree of coherence; incomplete; incomprehensible.

5 = highest level, 1 = lowest level

Figure 2
Checklist for Judging Richness of Retellings

	5	4	3	2	1
Generalizes beyond text	X				
Thesis (summarizing) statement	X	X			
Major points	X	X	X	?	?
Supporting details	X	X	X	X	?
Supplementations	Relevant	Relevant	Relevant	Irrelevant	Irrelevant
Coherence	High	Good	Adequate	Some	Poor
Completeness	High	Good	Adequate	Some	Poor
Comprehensibility	High	Good	Adequate	Some	Poor

The above matrix describes the evaluation of retellings in a holistic fashion on the basis of criteria (see Figure 1), similar to a procedure used to grade written compositions. This technique is an alternative to questioning for assessment of student comprehension of both narrative and expository text.

Ratings for both text types approximate bell-shaped curve distributions, but that for narrative text is skewed high, while that for expository text is skewed low. Since 12 different samples of each type of text were read and recalled, this may explain something about the differences in students' recall of the two text types rather than differences attributable to the judgments of the raters.

Irwin and Mitchell

Additional Raters

As a check on our procedures and to explore classroom use of the checklist in evaluating the richness of retellings, we asked members of a graduate reading seminar – 10 teachers with varying years and types of classroom experiences – to evaluate the 48 student retellings without knowing our assigned ratings. The teachers received instruction in use of the checklist but were not shown samples of retellings ranked by the 5 levels.

The teachers were given copies of the texts read by the 24 readers as well as transcriptions of the retellings. They were told to read each text and then its retelling. They were asked to read each retelling to gain a total impression of the student's comprehension, using the checklist to help them rate the retelling.

After the initial instruction, teachers' agreement with our ratings was only 38 percent. Teachers ranked about half the retellings of both narrative and expository text types below our assigned ratings. Teachers said their initial reactions to the transcribed retellings were similar to students' actual written work, which affected their expectations. Teachers also expressed a need for more specific guidance for rating. Subsequently, a second instructional session involved further discussion and clarification of the system, with examples of retellings which seemed particularly representative of each of the 5 levels.

The 48 retellings were again read and rated by the 10 teachers, following the same procedures. However, no retellings were rated by a teacher who had previously examined them. Exact agreement with our original ratings following this reading were 87.5 percent and when teacher ratings one level above or below our ratings were accepted as agreement, 100 percent agreement was achieved. The percent of agreement was identical for retellings of expository and narrative text types.

It is important to note that the high rating agreement between researchers and teachers followed a discussion of the 5 sets of retelling characteristics and the sharing of previously rated protocols, a step not unlike the anchoring procedure central to the holistic grading process used to evaluate written compositions. Since the steps were similar, it is not surprising that the percent of agreement for evaluating richness of retellings is consistent with that expected with use of holistic grading procedures.

While this checklist for judging the richness of retellings is still in an exploratory stage, our work has resulted in three interesting observations. First, retellings can be scored holistically rather than in terms of point accumulation reflecting value of their isolated parts. Second, this type of checklist can be used in evaluating retellings of both expository and narrative materials. Third, it is possible for teachers to use this system, provided that they have an opportunity to participate in group sessions, using the criteria for rating and examining samples of previously scored retellings.

Conclusion

Some cautions, of course, must be exercised in using the checklist to evaluate the richness of retellings. Retellings vary with such factors as (1) age, development, and proficiency of the reader; (2) form of retelling— oral vs. written, unaided vs. probed; and (3) text structure and content. Those using the checklist must be sensitive to the effects these factors may have on any given retelling.

Nevertheless, we believe that use of such a checklist provides a fresh way to look at reading comprehension through retellings. We therefore invite any interested person to join us in our exploratory research. Our goal is to gain additional insights into reader comprehension of text through the further development and refinement of an instrument which will adequately reflect the interaction between reader and text.

References

Bartlett, Frederic C. *Remembering: A Study in Experimental and Social Psychology.* Cambridge, England: Cambridge University Press, 1932.

Clark, Charles H. "Assessing Free Recall." *The Reading Teacher,* vol. 35 (January 1982), pp. 434-39.

Cooper, Charles R. "Holistic Evaluation of Writing." In *Evaluating Writing: Describing, Measuring, Judging,* edited by Charles R. Cooper and Lee Odell. Urbana, Ill.: National Council of Teachers of English, 1977.

Goodman, Yetta, and Carolyn L. Burke. *Reading Miscue Inventory—Manual.* New York, N.Y.: Macmillan, 1971.

Myers, Miles. *A Procedure for Writing Assessment and Holistic Scoring.* ED 193 676. Arlington, Va.: ERIC Document Reproduction Service, 1980.

Smith, Sharon L. "Assessing Student Learning and Retention Strategies Using Retellings of Text Passages." Report of the Learning Skills Center, Indiana University, 1980.

Smith, Sharon L. "Learning from Reading at the Secondary Level: An Investigation into Cognitive Operations Employed in the Reconstruction of Text." Doctoral dissertation, Indiana University, Bloomington, 1978.

GENERAL INSTRUCTIONAL STRATEGIES

Once the extent of student readiness for learning has been established through assessment, the teacher is better equipped to determine general instructional strategies. Has assessment revealed a wide range in the skills development of the whole class? Or does the whole class possess most of the skills required for successful content area learning, with only a few skills showing signs of general weakness? Besides revealing the pattern of skills development for the whole class, assessment also will show the pattern of strengths and weaknesses for individual students. Once these patterns have been established, the next step is to determine overall instructional strategies which will build on skills strengths, work toward strengthening skills weaknesses, and integrate teaching content with teaching the skills required to learn this content.

Integration is the key operating idea here. Little value for content area learning will derive from instruction which teaches reading and study skills in a vacuum, separate from students' direct and visible need for them. Here the learning principle of reinforcement in context must predominate over the principle of transfer to context. Experience shows that students have difficulty in making this transfer—they do not perceive the need for skills instruction when this instruction is separated from situations where they must apply skills directly for successful learning. It is therefore imperative that general instructional strategies be adopted which integrate the teaching of reading and study skills with the teaching of content.

The articles in this section are intended to provide guidance in achieving this integration. Their commonality lies in that each addresses a general instructional strategy which teachers can apply in their classrooms. Yet in every case, the creativity of the teacher is relied upon to convert these general strategies into living realities. None of these strategies should be undertaken in a rote fashion; to do so would invite failure and a return to the kind of unrealistic instruction which characterizes classrooms where students' reading needs are ignored. Rather, teachers should carefully assess what is being said in terms of their own particular teaching situation and content area. This is the only way the general guidelines provided can be translated into successful classroom practice.

The first article in the section bears witness to this fact. In it, Moore and Readence outline four approaches to content area reading instruction, each one different from the others, and yet each aimed at giving teachers a point of entry for introducing reading and study skill instruction in their classrooms. They wisely point out that there is almost no research to suggest the superiority of one approach over another and, therefore, classroom teachers (the real experts) are left to choose the approach with which they feel the most comfortable and which seems to promise the most success. In the second article, Harker elaborates on one of the approaches outlined by Moore and Readence, and thereby reveals his own prejudice based on his own classroom teaching experience. Next, Vacca discusses the importance of creating a context for learning before reading begins, and in doing so provides a valuable review of the relevant research supporting this strategy. Finally, in an excellent article held over from the first edition of this book, Earle and Sanders suggest ideas for individualizing instruction and thereby provide a realistic response to the almost certain range of individual differences which will be revealed by assessment.

- *What four general approaches to instruction are outlined?*
- *What are the strengths and the weaknesses of each approach?*

APPROACHES TO CONTENT AREA READING INSTRUCTION

David W. Moore
Indiana State University

John E. Readence
Louisiana State University

A crucial issue in content area reading instruction is how to instruct students so that they are able to study and learn from their texts. Text learning skills are needed at all grade levels, once content area instruction has begun. Educators need a clear perspective of possible approaches if they are to provide such instruction systematically at all levels.

In the related educational literature we find four basic approaches to teaching content area reading that are general enough to encompass primary grades as well as college level instruction. Each has advantages and disadvantages, discussed below. The fourth method attempts to give instruction in both the subject area and reading skills in an explicit and interrelated manner that has intrinsic appeal. However, there is no clear research support for the superiority of any of the four methods.

Presenting Isolated Skills

The first approach to showing students how to read their textbooks centers about the direct teaching of skills. It attempts to be content free. A specific set of skills, such as interpreting graphic aids, is identified and taught regardless of which learning tasks are currently confronting students in their texts.

The intent of direct, skills-centered instruction is to teach for transfer, so that students will later apply the skills independently as needed. The materials used are typically special items or workbooks unrelated to any content

Adapted from *Journal of Reading*, February 1983, *26*, 397-402.

being studied. Thus, students focus only on acquiring skills, using irrelevant content.

In essence, the isolated skills approach continues the method typically followed in beginning reading instruction, in that reading materials are selected only as a means to help students acquire targeted abilities. The major drawback is that students require help in transferring skills from one setting to another, and they often see little purpose in learning strategies divorced from content.

Aiming at Content

In a second approach, which we'll call "aiming," teachers focus students on learning the text's information, giving scant attention to informational acquiring skills. Aiming occurs as teachers direct students to particular aspects of the material that are to be learned. Purposes are set prior to reading; discussion to see whether students met them follows. Students are not told how to acquire or respond to information, but they are told what information to seek.

Aiming frequently occurs when students embark on their own research projects. In general, purposes for investigation are set in the form of problems to be solved, and students then explore a variety of sources to satisfy those purposes. Teachers help students focus their inquiry and locate information, but the emphasis usually is on students' independent reading.

Students require opportunities to read with teacher-directed purposes and on their own, to practice and reinforce skills and expand reading interests. However, controversy centers on whether aiming students toward content actually provides the skills. Stimulating students to read to solve problems and answer questions is seen by many as a necessary but insufficient condition for improving students' reading abilities.

Guiding toward Content

The third approach, "guiding," also directs students toward text information to be learned. However, the instruction is more structured than in "aiming." To guide students toward content, teachers first specify what knowledge they want acquired, and then they identify the necessary skills for learning it. A study guide is designed to lead students directly to desired text information; it also is meant to increase reading-learning abilities by modeling for students the process necessary to gather the appropriate information.

Study guides have much to offer, but they also have potential drawbacks, particularly in the way they are generally used in classrooms. Students who continually read to satisfy teacher-directed purposes and who use study guides regularly may learn much about a specific topic, but they risk becoming dependent on others to help them learn from text. Always guiding students is thought to help them acquire habits of searching for meaning—in time, they should expect automatically to learn from what they read. However, it is important to realize that both aiming and guiding students to content does not explicitly point out reading-learning strategies to them. Although some students may become aware of strategies and apply them independently following constant, guided use, acquiring learning skills or knowledge occurs best when the teacher focuses attention directly on the phenomena to be learned (Travers, 1977).

Aiming and guiding students' reading certainly are worthwhile activities, because they lead students directly to specified information. Teachers are responsible for helping students acquire vast amounts of facts and generalizations. However, training students to acquire information on their own is equally important. To quote an aphorism: "Give me a fish, and I eat for a day. Teach me to fish, and I eat for a lifetime."

Presenting Content and Skills Concurrently

Presenting content and skills concurrently is designed both to provide direct skills instruction and to guide students to selected information in text. The products of learning—the subject matter facts and generalizations—are stressed alongside the processes of learning—the skills to acquire facts and generalizations. This differs from the simultaneous approach embraced in study guides, which focus on product and process at the same point in time.

When presenting content and skills concurrently, teachers might decide that organizing subject matter into a main idea/detail format is necessary to learn certain content. If so, teachers might provide a lesson in organizing information according to a main idea/detail model before presenting the content. Students' attention to learning strategies is juxtaposed to attention to content. The learning strategy is made explicit for students. This approach follows Herber's notion of simulation (Herber, 1970, 1978), and it is evident in suggestions by McCallister (1936).

There are three effective procedures for providing concurrent content and skills instruction.

1. *Simulating* consists of giving students certain rules for learning from text. For example, Brown, Campione, and Day (1981) sketch a set of rules for summarizing passages, such as locating topic sentences, inventing topic sentences, and substituting general terms for lists of specifics. These summarization rules might be presented first to students with practice materials as a simulation of what to do when they read subject matter materi-

als. Next, students would apply the rules to summarize specific information to be learned from relevant content materials.

Supplementary skills materials that might be useful for the simulating procedure are *Go: Reading in the Content Areas* (Herber, 1975) and *Be a Better Reader* (Smith, 1969). Students might work through a selection in one of these which presents the process of inferring main ideas and their supporting details. After this priming, students would read their own subject matter and apply the learning strategy that had just been taught. Extra practice in noting main ideas/details is given to them later to reinforce and extend their use of the strategy. Materials may be supplementary readings or the actual content being covered in class.

2. *Debriefing* entails introspection, hindsight, and self-reports. For example, consider students' involvement in the Guided Reading Procedure or GRP (Manzo, 1975). Students read a text passage, record their unaided recalls, and organize these in some type of outline. They also verify what they recall and make necessary additions or corrections. The teacher directs this process by asking questions throughout the procedure, and short-term recall can be tested at the end.

In order to convert GRP and any other guiding or aiming procedure to a concurrent skills-content procedure, teachers debrief students as a follow up—that is, they question the students to obtain useful information about how the students had carried out the task.

The debriefing session helps students to crystallize the reading-learning processes involved in what they have just accomplished. Teachers might use the following probes to illuminate students' strategies in learning from text: how did you realize that some information was missing? How did you know some information was incorrect? How did you decide what seems to be the most important information? How did you decide what information supported the most important ideas? Might this be useful means to help you read and learn from other text reading assignments? Through such questioning, students become aware of processes that are available to learn content and, therefore, the processes they might employ later in learning from other texts.

Having students share their strategies this way is a time honored approach currently receiving much attention among educators involved with training students in problem solving (see Heiman, 1982). Study guides, if used as prescribed by Herber (1970, 1978), do involve some debriefing if the teacher conducts a follow-up session with students on the reading or reasoning processes involved in the guide.

(3) *Fading* happens when teachers first present students clear guidance in studying text but then gradually diminish guidance until students assume responsibility for their own learning. The goal is for students to become able to generate their own questions, thereby bringing about independent comprehension and learning of text.

A tactic that involves fading the guidance provided by questions is described by Moore, Readence, and Rickelman (1982). This tactic is based in part on models described by Singer (1978) and Herber and Nelson (1975). It rests on the belief that students should learn to direct their own reading independently by generating questions before, during, and after reading.

The first step in fading questions consists of teachers modeling good questioning behaviors. This entails taking students through text reading assignments, showing them appropriate questions to ask, and modeling the thinking process involved in designing questions. The traditional Directed Reading Activity format would be useful for modeling questions.

The second step occurs when teachers encourage and supervise students as they formulate their own questions about text. A straightforward tactic is to have individuals exchange questions and answers ping-pong style. First, one person asks a question about a passage, and another person answers it. The second person then asks a question, and the first person answers it. This question-answer exchange continues until the text information is exhausted. Teachers take part in these sessions in order to model good questioning behavior. The reciprocal questioning tactic described by Manzo (1969) is a formalized version of this type of lesson.

The third step in question fading consists of students conducting their own inquiry into content materials without teacher intervention. The Survey Technique (Aukerman, 1972) is useful for helping students initiate their own questions prior to reading. After reading, students might ask the teacher about any information in a passage, or they might form small groups and brainstorm possible questions for an upcoming quiz about a passage.

The concurrent skills-content approach is designed to move students toward independence in learning. Studies on metacognition have reemphasized and refined attention to this concern, and have shown that students can be taught directly how to learn (Brown, 1980). Concurrent skills-content instruction attempts to accomplish that. Perhaps the major problem with this approach is coordinating specific skills and content. Teachers must be able to determine the special reading assignment and provide a lesson that develops those strategies.

Summary

We have presented four approaches to content reading instruction. The first, presenting isolated skills, emphasizes the process of learning but ignores the products. Students attend to skills such as noting main idea/detail patterns of text organization, but the skills are not applied directly to learning relevant subject matter. Students on their own need to transfer skills from one situation to another. Conversely, aiming students toward content stresses the products of learning but ignores the processes. Students are directed toward some specific aspects of information that are available in books, but they then are left to their own devices to acquire that information.

Third, guiding students toward content is an enlightened form of aiming. Students focus on learning subject matter, but they are led to it and carefully helped to acquire teacher-specified information. Study guidance attempts to walk students through the reading-learning processes and ways to respond that are necessary for learning the content. However, as generally used in classroom situations, no direct attention is focused on those learning processes.

Finally, presenting skills and content concurrently happens when teachers emphasize learning skills alongside subject matter. Students are shown explicitly how to learn from their text. Their attention is directed at one time toward how to acquire information, and at another time toward the information itself. Skills are presented directly but in conjunction with content; they are not presented in isolation, nor are they elicited indirectly by providing guidance.

Which approach is best? There is no available research evidence to answer that question. Practically no studies have investigated the transfer effects of specific comprehension instruction on students' abilities to comprehend new, unfamiliar materials on their own (Jenkins & Pany, 1981; Tierney & Cunningham, 1980). In addition, answers to such a question are nearly impossible to obtain because too many factors go into implementing an approach. Rigorously following a single approach rarely happens because each one offers much room for variation. Indeed, we have emphasized general programs for delivering instruction, not specific, step-by-step lesson plan sequences. Finally, "Best for which students?" is a whole other question.

Because of the problems in determining which approach is best, teachers should examine the types of content area reading instruction presented here to determine which approach offers the most promise with regard to the resources available to them and the outcomes that are expected. With one or more of these approaches as a model, content area reading at least can occur systematically.

References

Aukerman, Robert C. *Reading in the Secondary Classroom.* New York, N.Y.: McGraw-Hill, 1972.

Brown, Ann L. "Metacognitive Development and Reading." In *Theoretical Issues in Reading Comprehension,* edited by Rand J. Spiro, Bertram C. Bruce, and William F. Brewer, pp. 453-81. Hillsdale, N.J.: Lawrence Erlbaum Associates, 1980.

Brown, Ann L., Joseph C. Campione, and Jeanne D. Day. "Learning to Learn: On Training Students to Learn from Texts." *Educational Researcher,* vol. 10 (February 1981), pp. 14-21.

Heiman, Marcia., ed. *Journal of Learning Skills,* vol. 1 (Winter 1982), entire issue.

Herber, Harold L. *Teaching Reading in the Content Areas.* Englewood Cliffs, N.J.: Prentice-Hall, 1970.

Herber, Harold L. *Go: Reading in the Content Areas.* New York, N.Y.: Scholastic, 1975.

Herber, Harold L., and Joan B. Nelson. "Questioning Is Not the Answer." *Journal of Reading,* vol. 18 (April 1975), pp. 512-17.

Jenkins, Joseph R., and Darlene Pany. "Instructional Variables in Reading Comprehension." In *Comprehension and Teaching: Research Reviews,* edited by John T. Guthrie, pp. 203-226. Newark, Del.: International Reading Association, 1981.

Manzo, Anthony V. "Guided Reading Procedure." *Journal of Reading,* vol. 18 (January 1975), pp. 287-91.

Manzo, Anthony V. "The ReQuest Procedure." *Journal of Reading,* vol. 13 (November 1969), pp. 123-26, 163.

McCallister, James M. *Remedial and Corrective Instruction in Reading.* New York, N.Y.: Appleton-Century, 1936.

Moore, David W., John E. Readence, and Robert J. Rickelman. *Prereading Activities for Content Area Reading and Learning.* Newark, Del.: International Reading Association, 1982.

Singer, Harry. "Active Comprehension: From Answering to Asking Questions." *Reading Teacher,* vol. 31 (May 1978), pp. 901-08.

Smith, Nila B. *Be a Better Reader,* 3rd ed. Englewood Cliffs, N.J.: Prentice-Hall, 1969.

Tierney, Robert J., and James W. Cunningham. *Research on Teaching Reading Comprehension.* Technical Report No. 187. Urbana, Ill.: Center for the Study of Reading, University of Illinois, 1980.

Travers, Robert M.W. *Essentials of Learning,* 4th ed. New York, N.Y.: Macmillan, 1977.

203727

- *What four steps are outlined to ensure the integration of skills and content?*
- *How can this procedure be modified to meet teaching requirements in different content areas?*

DOES CONTENT AREA READING TEACH CONTENT AREA LEARNING?

W. John Harker
University of Victoria

The 1970s may be called the decade of content area reading. From tentative beginnings in the 1960s and before, content area reading instruction has gained recognition during the 1970s as an effective means of furthering students' learning in the content areas.

But what real progress has been made? To what extent has content area reading instruction actually furthered students' content area learning? The answer seems to be equivocal. While there has been a growing acceptance by teachers of reading and study skills as important aspects of school learning (Jackson, 1979), a closer look at the directions for instruction given to teachers suggests that there remains considerable confusion over the purpose and practice of content-area reading.

This confusion is best exemplified in a number of recent textbooks dealing with teaching reading in the content areas (Dillner & Olson, 1977; Forgan & Mangrum, 1976; Piercey, 1976; Robinson, 1978; Thomas and Robinson, 1977). These textbooks all provide specific guidance in planning and implementing content area reading activities. But they fail to link these activities with particular content area learning objectives. Teachers are left to assume that somehow by teaching a wide range of isolated reading and study skills, content area learning will be improved.

This assumption is open to question. It is reminiscent of the experience of remedial teachers who find retarded readers becoming increasingly proficient at performing the tasks required by various remedial programs, but remaining unable to handle assignments in reading outside these programs. Similarly, teaching content area reading activities detached from a clear

Adapted from *Reading Horizons*, Fall 1981, *22*, 25-28. Used by permission.

determination of the specific content area learning which these activities are intended to improve will fail to result in student gains in content area learning. The following four steps are suggested to teachers as a way of ensuring that content area reading instruction does in fact teach content area learning.

Step 1: *Determining Content Area Learning Objectives*

Content area learning objectives define what the teacher considers important for students to learn. The question for the teacher to ask is, "What is it about my content area (geography, English, science, etc.) that I can realistically expect my students to gain from my teaching, given the resources and limitations under which we both must work?" For example, in a unit or lesson in geography, the content area objective may be that students gain an understanding of how a watershed forms; in English, the objective may be an understanding of the ways in which a short story writer develops character through dialogue; or in science, the objective may be an understanding of the periodic table of the elements.

Step 2: *Determine Needed Reading and Study Skills*

Besides determining what content area learning will be pursued, content area objectives have the second function of defining the specific reading and study skills needed for their achievement. It is only after content area learning objectives have been specifically determined that the particular reading and study skills needed by students for the achievement of these objectives can be identified.

This identification can be done through introspection. The teacher will "think through" the content area task of learning from the students' point of view, taking such factors under consideration as students' previous learning, their general level of achievement, and the degree of mastery to be expected. This is both a difficult and a crude method, but next to directly observing students' thinking while learning—a desirable but up to now impossible practice—teacher introspection is the best method available. For example, in "thinking through" the learning task presented to students in understanding how a watershed forms, the teacher may identify such needed skills as map reading, making predictions, and determining relationships of cause and effect.

Step 3: *Diagnosis*

The next step is for the teacher to determine which skills students already possess and which ones need to be taught. For example, the English teacher who wants to know the level of students' preparedness to understand how a short story writer develops character through dialogue will prepare an informal test based on short story material with questions measuring the students' ability to perform the skills they need to gain this understanding. These skills might include such ones as identifying significant details, visualization, and interpreting connotative language. When students' ability to perform these skills has been assessed, the teacher will know in which skills areas students are weak, with specific reference to the particular content area learning objective intended for instruction. In this way, subsequent skills teaching can focus directly on the exact areas of need thereby avoiding wasting time teaching skills which are not supportive of the specific content area learning objective being pursued, or which students have already mastered. A number of writers have provided teachers with comprehensive directions in the preparation of group information tests, and these sources can be referred to for further guidance (Ahrendt & Haselton, 1973; Rakes, 1975; Shepherd, 1978; Taschow, 1967; and Voix, 1968).

Step 4: *Skills Selection*

An obvious outcome of diagnostic teaching is that not all skills are taught all the time. For example, the science teacher whose content area objective in learning is that students gain an understanding of the periodic table of the elements will not concentrate on word attack skills since the information to be understood is presented by symbols (therefore making the comprehension of symbols a skill which will be assessed and taught if necessary), the level of comprehension required is literal (therefore making teaching critical and inferential levels of comprehension [Harker, 1973] unnecessary—although in teaching students to apply the information once comprehended, these levels of comprehension will probably be required).

The point is that teachers will not attempt to instruct students in the full range of the reading and study skills at any one time. But instruction in this range will ultimately result as students encounter skills instruction in the different content areas as the need for this instruction arises through the academic levels. And since this instruction will be in direct response to specific content area learning objectives, the teaching of these skills will be highly functional, rather than being in some undefined way "comprehensive" with little or no direct reference to specific objectives.

Conclusion

In answer to the question, "Does content area reading teach content area learning?" the answer is "Yes" if teachers keep in mind the real purpose for teaching reading and study skills in the content areas. This purpose is not to "get through" an arbitrary list of skills which has application to content area learning in at best only a general sense. The purpose, rather, is to provide students with the specific skills of reading and study they require to achieve clearly defined content area learning objectives. These objectives are the ones which content area teachers have traditionally pursued, and which they have also seen as being intruded upon by reading and study skill instruction. It is probably the most important development of the 1970s for teachers of content area reading that there is less likelihood now of viewing reading and study skill instruction as an intrusion, but that they are willing to admit the value of this instruction in furthering content area learning. However, the direction currently being given teachers to teach content area reading and study skills having no direct link to content area learning objectives threatens to reverse this progress.

References

Ahrendt, Kenneth M. "Informal Skills Assessment for Individualized Instruction." *Journal of Reading,* October 1973, *17,* 52-57.

Dillner, Martin, H., and Olson, Joanne P. *Personalizing Reading Instruction in Middle, Junior, and Senior High Schools.* New York: Macmillan, 1977.

Forgan, Harry W., and Mangrum, Charles T. *Teaching Content Area Reading Skills.* Columbus: Merrill, 1976.

Harker, W. John. "Teaching Comprehension: A Task Analysis Approach." *Journal of Reading,* February 1973, *16,* 379-382.

Hill, Walter R., *Secondary School Reading.* Boston: Allyn and Bacon, 1979.

Jackson, James E. "Reading in the Secondary School: A Survey of Teachers." *Journal of Reading,* December 1979, *23,* 229-232.

Piercey, Dorothy. *Reading Activities in Content Areas.* Boston: Allyn and Bacon, 1978.

Shepherd, David. *Comprehensive High School Reading Methods,* 2nd ed. Columbus: Merrill, 1978.

Taschow, Horst G. "Instructional Reading Levels in Subject Matter Areas." *Reading Improvement,* 1967, *4,* 73-76.

Thomas, Ellen Lamar, and Robinson, H. Alan. *Improving Reading in Every Class,* 2nd ed. Boston: Allyn and Bacon, 1977.

Voix, Ruth G. *Evaluating Reading and Study Skills in the Secondary Classroom.* Newark, Del: International Reading Association, 1968.

- *What is a structured overview and how does it provide readiness for learning?*
- *Why is it important to present the structured overview before reading begins?*

READINESS TO READ CONTENT AREA ASSIGNMENTS

Richard T. Vacca
Kent State University

There's a consensus among reading people that readiness should be a practical part of reading instruction at every teaching level. Karlin (1964, p. 236), for example, agrees that while the readiness concept has been applied to primary reading, "its influences may be felt at each instructional level." The goal of readiness to read in content areas presumes that students will be mentally and psychologically prepared to begin a reading assignment—in a state of mind which will promote learning.

As a general principle, readiness refers to the ability of an individual at a given age to cope adequately with the demands of a cognitive task (Ausubel, 1963). Frederick's review (1968, p. 18) of research on readiness activities generally indicates that, "Pre-learning experiences can be used to advantage in readiness if experiences: 1) lead to a concept, 2) are relevant to the concept, and 3) provide a direction in learning the concept." Ausubel (1963) argues that there is little disagreement that readiness always crucially affects the efficiency of the learning process. He indicates, however, that little if any significant research has been conducted in the classroom. As far as readiness for reading is concerned, Marksheffel (1966) reiterates that it is intrinsic to reading at every instructional level, but admits that it has received "insufficient attention and is little understood" by reading personnel.

Since the 1960s, however, readiness to learn through written discourse has been analyzed from many investigative perspectives. Insights have emerged; promising instructional procedures have been introduced into the literature.

Adapted from *Journal of Reading*, February 1977, *20*, 387-392.

In particular, a great deal of experimental activity has focused on Ausubel's theory (1963, 1968) of "meaningful reception learning." It's appropriate, therefore, to consider the developments arising from this theory and the implications they have for those content teachers who themselves are "ready" to expand their instructional repertoires.

First, however, consider the following review of where the reading field has been with readiness-to-read methodology. This will provide a framework in which to understand better the implications of meaningful reception learning for readiness to read in content areas.

Readiness to Read in Retrospect

Part of the readiness concept states that individuals must know certain things before they can learn specific, additional materials, or that they must develop certain skills before they can develop others. Because readiness is an inferred mental state, teachers unfortunately have little direct knowledge of an individual's state of readiness. Nevertheless, through detailed knowledge of a student's educational background and the use of diagnostic tools, fairly shrewd inferences can be made about readiness for a specific reading task.

Classroom teachers in elementary schools attempt to ensure children's readiness by giving them preparatory activities. These procedures have become traditional. In reading methods textbooks or basal teaching manuals, lesson formats typically espouse a "readiness stage" which emphasizes in one way or another: 1) setting purposes, 2) building background and experiences, and 3) teaching unfamiliar vocabulary. The same steps can be applied at all grade levels and in all content areas.

If taken at face value, these activities usually are beguiling to the unsuspecting teacher. Armed with an undergraduate or graduate course in reading (if any at all), he/she may begin classes with the idea that a dash of new vocabulary here and a sprinkling of questions there will suffice in preparing readers for the learning task ahead. Obviously this is an oversimplification of readiness methodology. Nevertheless, much more than the routine of a readiness stage is needed to prepare students.

A structure is needed that will help learners link what they know with what they will study. Herber (1970), in discussing how a teacher can structure a lesson through which both content and reading can be taught, elaborates on the stage of preparing the student for the lesson. In Herber's instructional framework, preparation presumes the necessity of cognitive readiness and has several interdependent elements:

1) Motivation
2) Background information and review
3) Anticipation and purpose
4) Direction
5) Language development

1) Content teachers use those motivational techniques which best fit their style and personality. They determine which approach actually will arouse a particular group of students for a specific lesson. The witty start, the dramatic presentation, the novel prelearning experience are all useful in sparking excitement or curiosity about the material to be read.

2) As students get set for the reading task, they need a frame of reference for the concepts they will encounter and acquire. Background information helps build this framework, providing a context into which new information can be fitted. There is a need to review common experiences and relate them to the subject matter, to enlarge and strengthen the context of the topics which the students will be dealing with in the reading assignment.

With respect to this frame of reference, one of Stauffer's criticisms (1969, p. 53) of the readiness activities of basal readers should be heeded. He questions whether a brief, teacher-directed talk session ever "builds" experiences or leads to concept development: "Will talking about a hungry lion...or a circus or an Indian build concepts?"

Similarly, a social studies teacher once spoke of her experience with an eighth grade class on the island of Guam. She was teaching about the coal resources of the U.S.A. During her readiness period, she wished to clear up possible confusion by telling students that *coke* was not to be mistaken for a popular soft drink. She then spent several weeks on the unit using pictures, projects, reports and the like. Finally, she gave a test in which one pupil, responding to a particular question, wrote, "I know coke is made from coal—but it still tastes good." Clearly, as Stauffer (1975, p. 9) suggests, "Concepts are not acquired by artificial explanations and compulsory memorization, but by giving students a chance to acquire them in, by, and through their functional contexts."

3) During the preparation period, teachers try to help students anticipate what they'll be dealing with and set a purpose for their reading. The essential question, however, is, "Set whose purpose?" Students'? Teacher's? How does a teacher reconcile his/her purpose(s) with those of students who may have no particular interest in the topic? According to Herber (1970, pp. 33-34) students establish reading purposes through the structure provided by the teacher:

The structure provided by the teacher should reflect his own preparation for the lesson: he has determined the ideas he believes are important enough for students to acquire. He encourages pupils to be receptive to those ideas as they read. He also determines how the students must read the material in order to develop those ideas, and he gives students direction in the application of those ideas. Consequently, students read for the purpose of developing specific ideas, and they do so with a conscious application of specific, appropriate skills.

4) Another part of ensuring readiness to read is that content teachers give students directions as to specific skills which they will need in order to handle the subject matter in their next unit. Since these skills differ according to the subject, the teacher must analyze the reading material to determine which will be needed.

5) Finally, teachers prepare readers for the technical vocabulary they will encounter. Students should become familiar with key vocabulary and gain a degree of facility with it before they read.

In retrospect the preparatory aspects of readiness to read should help students to link the "given"—what they already know or the skills that they have—with the "new"—what they are about to learn. The bulk of effective "reading instruction" in the content areas may very well come before students read—during the preparation component of a teacher's lesson. Hansell (1976, p. 309) accurately states,

Teachers may help students to read texts, articles, or books by helping them understand the content before they deal with it in print…the problem of content teachers then becomes, in the words of an eighth grade teacher in Boston, one of "convincing the students that they know more than they think they do about my subject."

Since the 1960s research involving "meaningful reception learning" has introduced a number of developments affecting cognitive readiness. These developments do not require classroom teachers to alter drastically what they already know about preparing students to read. Rather, they can be adapted to the procedures described above. In this way content area teachers are in a position to increase their instructional repertoires and approach readiness from a wider intellectual perspective.

Basing their work on Ausubel's belief that an individual's wealth of knowledge is organized hierarchically in terms of highly generalized concepts, less inclusive concepts, and specific facts, experimenters have studied extensively the use of "advance organizers" as an aid to learning and retaining concepts. Advance organizers attempt to maximize the cognitive readiness of learners prior to a new task. Ausubel maintains that cognitive structure—"an individual's organization, stability, and clarity of knowledge in a particular subject-matter field at any given time"—is a major factor in learning and retention. Learning is facilitated to the extent that previous knowledge is clear, stable, and organized.

Ausubel suggests that advance organizers, if constructed and used properly, would enhance learning and aid retention because they tend to clarify and organize an individual's cognitive structure prior to a learning task. Advance organizers presumably contain the necessary relevant "subsuming concepts" which enable learners to fit new meaning into previous frameworks.

An advance organizer, then, is defined by Ausubel (1968, p. 214) as preparatory paragraphs which provide:

> Relevant ideational scaffolding, enhance the discriminability of the new learning material from previously learned related ideas, and otherwise effect integrative reconciliation at a level of abstraction, generality, and inclusiveness which is much higher than the learning material itself. To be maximally effective they must be formulated in terms of language, concepts, propositions already familiar to the learner, and use appropriate illustrations and analogies.

Baker (1976) has reviewed fifty-two published research reports dealing with Ausubel's theory of meaningful reception learning. His exhaustive review establishes that the majority of studies conducted *since* Ausubel's investigations have been nonsupportive. More than two-thirds of the studies, though, are short term, "one shot" experiments rather than prolonged investigations. Moreover, more than twenty different forms of advance organizers have been investigated.

One of the major limitations of advance organizer research has been the lack of a commonly accepted operational definition that allows for careful replication. Baker suggests future studies could profit from a detailed analysis of Ausubel's theoretical base, rather than on his specific treatment— the advance organizer.

A structured overview is a preparatory activity which has its roots in Ausubel's theoretical base of meaningful reception learning (Barron, 1969). More and more it is mentioned in the literature on reading instruction (Catterson, 1974; Manzo, 1975; Hansell, 1976). Thus far, the International Reading Association has published two monographs in its Reading Aids Series which serve as excellent content area reading resources for math and science teachers. Both monographs (Earle, 1976; Thelen, 1984) provide a description and numerous examples of the structured overview adapted as a readiness procedure in math and science classes.

Structured overviews are visual diagrams of the key vocabulary of a learning task "in relation to more inclusive or subsuming vocabulary concepts that have been previously learned by the student" (Estes & others, 1969, p. 41). Earle (1969) devised a set of directions to make the construction of overviews a non-time consuming and realistic task for teachers:

1. Select every word that you intend to use in a unit that you think is necessary to the students' understanding what you want them to understand.
2. Take the list of words and arrange them and rearrange them until you have a diagram which shows the relationships which exist among the ideas in the unit.
3. Use an overhead or write the diagram on the chalkboard the first day of the lesson (or use as a prelearning experience before students read). Explain why you arranged the words the way you did and have students contribute as much information as possible.

The figure represents a structured overview that was constructed by Joseph Janoch, a ninth grade social studies teacher from Lyons Township High School, LaGrange, Illinois. Note the hierarchy of major concepts, their connection to one another, in the reading selection. The social studies teacher has an opportunity to preteach key technical terms, draw upon students' understandings and experiences with the terms. Possibly the teacher will have students relate several of the terms to previous study or learnings within the course. Furthermore, notice the implicit comparison-contrast pattern expressed in the structured overview. What better way to provide directions for the needed reading skills that will be applied to this selection than to have students visualize it through the diagram! The structured overview provides a visual map, a network, that permits students to see the relatedness of the important concepts in an overall unit or specific reading assignment to be studied.

Structured Overview: Social Studies Unit

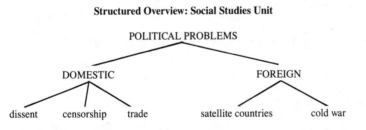

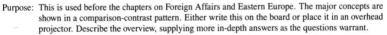

Purpose: This is used before the chapters on Foreign Affairs and Eastern Europe. The major concepts are shown in a comparison-contrast pattern. Either write this on the board or place it in an overhead projector. Describe the overview, supplying more in-depth answers as the questions warrant.

The structured overview thus can become an important preparatory tool in the perception of relationships and the acquisition of concepts. In addition, it may very well have an additional "side benefit." After continued use of the structured overview in a classroom setting, Earle (1969, p. 53) notes the reaction of one teacher: "Preparing and using the overview made my teaching easier. I knew exactly where I was going...." The structured overview, then, is a way of helping classroom teachers to clarify their content objectives and to identify precisely the major ideas to be encountered and acquired by students.

References

Ausubel, D.P. *Educational Psychology—A Cognitive View.* New York, N.Y.: Holt, Rinehart and Winston, 1968.

Ausubel, D.P. *The Psychology of Meaningful Verbal Learning.* New York, N.Y.: Grune & Stratton, 1963.

Baker, R.L. "Meaningful Reception Learning." *Research in Reading in the Content Areas: Third Year Report.* H.L. Herber and R.T. Vacca, Eds. Syracuse, N.Y.: Syracuse University Reading and Language Arts Center, 1977.

Barron, R.F. "The Use of Vocabulary as an Advance Organizer." *Research in Reading in the Content Areas: First Year Report.* H.L. Herber and P.L. Sanders, Eds. Syracuse, N.Y.: Syracuse University Reading and Language Arts Center, 1969.

Catterson, J.H. "Techniques for Improving Comprehension in Mathematics." *Reading in the Middle School.* G.G. Duffy, Ed. pp. 153-65. Newark, Del.: International Reading Association, 1974.

Earle, R.A. *Teaching Reading and Mathematics.* Newark, Del.: International Reading Association, 1976.

Earle, R.A. "Use of Structured Overview in Mathematics Classes." *Research in Teaching Reading in the Content Areas: First Year Report.* H.L. Herber and P.L. Sanders, Eds. Syracuse, N.Y.: Syracuse University Reading and Language Arts Center, 1969.

Estes, T.H. and others. "Three Methods of Introducing Students to a Reading-Learning Task in Two Content Subjects." *Research in Reading in the Content Areas: First Year Report.* H.L. Herber and P.L. Sanders, Eds. Syracuse, N.Y.: Syracuse University Reading and Language Arts Center, 1969.

Frederick, E.C. A Study of the Effects of Readiness Activities on Concept Learning. Unpublished doctoral dissertation. Syracuse University, 1968.

Hansell, T.S. "Increasing Understanding in Content Reading." *Journal of Reading,* vol. 19, no. 4 (January 1976), pp. 307-11.

Herber, H.L. *Teaching Reading in Content Areas.* Englewood Cliffs, N.J.: Prentice-Hall, 1970.

Karlin, R. *Teaching Reading in High School.* 1st ed. Indianapolis, Ind.: Bobbs-Merrill, 1964.

Manzo, A.V. "Guided Reading Procedure." *Journal of Reading,* vol. 18, no. 4 (January 1975), pp. 287-91.

Marsheffel, N.A. *Better Reading in the Secondary School.* New York, N.Y.: Ronald Press Co., 1966.

Stauffer, R.G. *The Dimensions of Sound Reading Instruction.* Paper presented at the 25th Annual Reading Conference, University of Delaware, Newark, Delaware, 1975.

Stauffer, R.G. *Directing Reading Maturity as a Cognitive Process.* New York, N.Y.: Harper and Row, 1969.

Thelen, J. *Improving Reading in Science.* Newark, Del.: International Reading Association, 1984.

- *What are the six procedures described for individualizing reading assignments?*
- *How can these procedures be adapted to meet the specific needs of students in different content areas?*

INDIVIDUALIZING READING ASSIGNMENTS

Richard A. Earle
McGill University

Peter L. Sanders
Wayne State University

Any teacher who has spent more than a day or two in the public school classroom knows that students—whether they are grouped homogenously or not—represent considerable variation in the ability to read required text material. This range of reading ability, and the variety and difficulty of subject matter text, are obstacles which can prevent effective interaction between the student and the text. Those students who are fortunate enough to have attained independence may need no special help. But what about the others? Is it "sink or swim"?

A short informal assessment of reading ability will reveal which students are less than successful in mastering their reading. Even more important are the observations of a sensitive teacher, one who feels that if an assignment is worth giving at all, differential amounts of assistance must be provided for certain individuals and groups within the class.

Individualizing subject matter assignments is an attempt to get away from regarding a class as a monolithic "they." It means providing enough help to ensure that each student will successfully master the required reading. It does not require an individual preparation for each student in the class. Nor does it mean a different text for each individual. No one means should be singled out and used exclusively. In fact, various techniques may prove useful in different situations and in several combinations.

Levels of Sophistication

Not all students will find it possible to answer sophisticated questions requiring the application of meaning from subject matter reading. Some

Adapted from *Journal of Reading,* April 1973, *16,* 550-555.

students might well profit from questions designed to identify and generalize relationships among particular facts or ideas. By the same token, poorer readers generally find it easier to locate and verify answers to specific factual questions, rather than questions requiring interpretation or application.

This suggests the first means of individualizing subject matter reading assignments. Given an important assignment, match question difficulty to the student's reading ability. Thus, each student can experience the satisfaction of mastery at some level of comprehension, while all the essential information is gleaned from the assignment. Postreading classroom discussion can be planned to ensure that the information gained by each can be shared by all.

One note of caution: It is tempting to "pigeonhole" students using this method. We have been greeted (by teachers who *thought* they were individualizing) with such statements as "These are my literal level kids, these are my interpretation level kids, and these are my application level kids." A permanent classification such as implied in this statement is not desirable. It may be detrimental to the child's learning, certainly to his continued reading growth in the subject matter classroom. Regarded as one means of adjusting the task to student abilities, however, teacher questioning at different levels can represent useful and constructive assistance.

Differential Structuring

One of the most useful techniques for differentiating subject matter reading assignments is to ask questions or give instructions which incorporate various degrees of structure, according to the needs of different students or groups of students. "Structure" in this case means guidance built into the question itself. For example, a teacher whose "guidance" consists only of "Read Chapter 7 for tomorrow" is really saying to the students, "Some important questions about our subject matter are answered in this reading assignment, but I'm not going to tell you what questions they are. You find the answers, come in tomorrow, and in our discussion I'll let you know what the questions were. If your answers fit my questions, you will be a winner; if not, you lose."

Considerable guidance can be provided by a simple question, for example, "Read this assignment to find out such and such." While this at least provides students with some purpose for attacking the reading assignment, some students will have difficulty in locating and verifying such information, particularly in a lengthy reading assignment. For these students, a somewhat higher level of structure is in order.

Our experience suggests that reacting to alternatives is in fact easier than generating alternatives. Therefore, questions can be structured with several possible answers, the student's task being to verify one or more of the alternatives provided. Depending on the student's need for structure, alternatives can be sophisticated statements representing application, generalization, or inference, each to be supported or refuted with evidence from the reading.

On the other hand, several important details can be included in a structured question, with the student being required to verify their literal existence in the text. In some cases students who are unable to read well enough to comprehend material in paragraph and/or sentence form can be supplied with a list of single words to be verified or rejected in the light of a particular subject matter question. Combined with these techniques, even more structure can be provided by giving locational aid in the form of page and/or column number.

Some students who are overwhelmed by several pages of reading can succeed when the teacher indicates the paragraph (or even the line number) where the information can be found. This approach—like most other elements of individualizing—depends on the difficulty the students are likely to have with a given assignment. It is interesting to note that some students who are labeled "nonreaders" have successfully read this subject matter assignments when questions included a little more structure. Structuring a question differentially means providing, within the question itself, enough guidance so that the student is more certain of locating, identifying, and verifying essential information contained in a reading assignment.

Collaboration by Grouping

There is an old saying that "Two heads are better than one." This particular approach to individualizing rests on the tenet that, with some reading assignments, three, four, or five heads are better than one. The essential element of collaboration is teamwork—the sharing of information and skills in order to get the job done. Several forms of grouping allow the sort of team sharing that is the essence of group collaboration.

One is what we would call a "tutor" group, where one person who has a superior skill in reading can be teamed with one or more students who are not as effective. The tutor, with some direction from the teacher, might read portions of the assignment to the others, clarify directions, react to their answers, and generally provide needed assistance. In some cases, two readers of equal ability might help each other, combining information to arrive at a larger understanding than either could achieve alone. Another form of grouping is "ability" grouping, where the class is divided into two or more groups representing different levels of reading performance.

This sort of grouping, while not recommended as permanent, is particularly useful when combined with the technique of questioning at different levels of comprehension. Still another form of grouping is "interest" grouping, where students are teamed to complete various tasks representing common interests.

Incidentally, most students, given the choice, will not select a task that appears too easy; rather, they will elect to do that which is both interesting and challenging.

Perhaps the most common form of useful collaboration in the subject matter classroom can be achieved by "random" grouping. In this form of grouping two or more students are teamed on the basis of any random means, such as their seating arrangements in the classroom. As with other forms of collaboration, the object here is to share skills and information. However, the most important element of random grouping is that it encourages an interaction among the students. In contrast to the teacher-led classroom discussion, random grouping provides each student time and opportunity to verbalize his findings, support his generalization, and question other students.

Students are sometimes uneasy or even amused by the prospect of collaborative effort. Certainly they have little opportunity for such sharing in many classrooms throughout their public school career. And the teacher may feel uneasy, perhaps equating group collaboration with cheating or improper teaching. However, two facts should be made clear regarding grouping: 1) Students *do* learn from each other by assisting or challenging their colleagues in active ways; 2) Teachers, when freed from the total absorption demanded by the lecture, are able to help, stimulate, and evaluate students in individual ways. If you regard group effort as an integral part of individualized learning, your students will catch on very quickly. Collaboration on subject matter assignments is one effective way of improving learning, especially for the less effective reader.

Selecting Appropriate Material

In the ideal classroom, each student operates with material that is suited to his instructional level. We know however that this ideal is rarely the case. Some subject matter simply cannot be presented at low levels of difficulty. In other cases, money is not available to buy published materials. Or a given textbook may be required by those who design the curriculum. The net result is that most content classrooms boast a single textbook, often too

Earle and Sanders

difficult for the student. This situation necessitates other methods of individualizing, such as mentioned in this article. Nonetheless, when curriculum-specific materials of easier readability are available, they become another excellent means of providing each student in your class with the opportunity to master his reading assignment successfully.

Vary Assignment Length

In classrooms where coverage of the entire course takes precedence over student understanding, there is little opportunity to expect more of some students than of others. However, some teachers feel that mastery of fewer understandings is more important than superficial coverage of large amounts of subject matter material. These teachers have found that yet another way to individualize is to vary their length, that is, the number of understandings to be gained. Some students can handle lengthy assignments satisfactorily. We know, however, that others are completely overwhelmed by the prospect of ten or twelve pages of text. Hence, they avoid the pain and frustration of failure by refusing to do the assignment at all. For these students, reducing the reading assignment to manageable proportions often gives them more opportunity for success. For example, some may be directed to read only the most important sections of the material, perhaps even a single page. Others may experience success in selecting a few of the important ideas or descriptive terms. In extreme cases poor readers could be asked to do no more than verify certain key words. This particular technique is particularly useful in conjunction with differential structuring of questions.

Many students need more time to complete required reading assignments. They might be more successful if given a few additional minutes (or hours) to complete the task. It is unfortunate that the usual public school organization—the forty-five minute class period, the eighteen week semester, and the graded year—makes this sort of basic individual assistance very difficult. Nevertheless, the subject matter teacher can devise means for adjusting the time factor in reading assignments while retaining the necessary degree of guidance and control. Many sensitive teachers endorse deadlines firmly but not rigidly; they do not regard deadlines as sacrosanct. Sometimes a straightforward question (for example, "Would it be helpful if you had till tomorrow, or next Monday?") can guide the teacher in his decision. Surely it would do wonders for the student-teacher relationship by communicating the concern and flexibility that is the hallmark of the sensitive teacher. Students who finish an assignment may move on to other tasks, including the task of helping those who need additional guidance. It is important to note that additional time must often be combined with other types of assistance, as suggested in this article.

It is difficult (even dangerous) for reading specialists to suggest publicly replacing printed text with assignments that do not require reading. However, the underlying premise of this article and the major concern of most subject teachers is that mastery of the subject matter takes precedence over a student's reading development.

In point of fact, the teacher is expected to teach subject matter ideas and skills regardless of students' reading abilities. Even when the student receives separate expert reading instruction, increased reading ability is a long time coming. Therefore, when the student is severely handicapped, many important ideas can be communicated through other media, such as pictures, tapes, records, films, filmstrips, and the like. Of course, we must face the fact that complete abandonment of required reading prevents the student from improving his reading ability. He becomes forever dependent on speech alone to gather and assess information in a given subject area. It therefore seems advisable to use other media as supplement rather than as replacement.

For example, material presented orally can often be accompanied by written questions structured to provide a maximum amount of guidance. Since the questions are in written form they will require reading; hence they represent elements integral to both subject matter mastery and continued reading growth. However, to the degree that reduction or abandonment of printed material is necessary to ensure student success, the technique can be effective in overcoming the obstacles presented by reading assignments.

Summary

This article has described several techniques for individualizing reading assignments in subject matter classes. The approaches mentioned herein do not represent a comprehensive list of suggestions. Nor are they all guaranteed to be equally practical, or equally comfortable to certain teachers. Experience suggests, however, that the use of these approaches has provided many "nonreaders" with the help they needed to become successful readers—at least to some degree. That alone may be reason enough to give them a try!

INSTRUCTIONAL MATERIALS

Placing this section after the one on general strategies gives recognition to an instructional ideal at the expense of a teaching reality. In the first place, an ideal of effective instruction is that the reading material from which students are expected to learn will be determined by the instructional objectives and strategies employed to bring about this learning. In other words, content area learning objectives and the general methods adopted to achieve these objectives will be determined first. Once this has been done, the instructional materials can be chosen. In this way, materials do not become the determiners of instruction but rather the facilitators of instruction. Teachers first decide what and how they will teach, and then proceed to select materials which will allow them to do this.

But what may be effective in theory may be impossible in practice owing to the pervasiveness of another reality. Rather than being free to choose the instructional materials considered most effective, teachers are often faced with using materials mandated by local or state and provincial agencies. And these agencies are notorious for failing to consult with the teachers whose professional responsibility it is to implement the materials mandated. In this situation, rather than instructional practice determining materials, materials come first, and the teachers' job becomes one of accommodating materials to the instructional objectives and methods which they wish to employ.

Ways by which this accommodation can be achieved are the subject of this section. The orientation here is that, although experience shows that the classroom teacher is seldom a free agent in materials selection, there are still ways in which the teacher can control and shape the use of mandated instructional materials. In the first article, Harker outlines five criteria which, when used together, can reveal the relative strengths and weaknesses of materials in order that they can be used to their optimum advantage and their shortcomings avoided. In the next article Fry, the author of one of the best known and most widely used formulas for determining the readability of instructional materials, updates his original formula and discusses some of the isssues which have arisen since its introduction. Following this, Nelson provides a reasoned commentary on the use of readability formulas in materials selected by content area teachers. Finally, Morrow explains the development of teacher made materials, and in doing so gives content area teachers a way of avoiding the worst excesses of situations where mandated materials may be either totally unusable or where they must be augmented.

- *What five criteria are given for evaluating content area instructional materials?*
- *How can the weighting of these criteria be altered to suit materials evaluation in different content areas?*

SELECTING INSTRUCTIONAL MATERIALS FOR CONTENT AREA READING

W. John Harker
University of Victoria

Content area instructional materials are learning devices, not just sources of content area information. When selecting instructional materials, it is necessary to ensure that they provide the information required for students to achieve content area learning objectives. But it is equally necessary to ensure that they do not frustrate students' learning by imposing barriers to reading and understanding.

This article presents five criteria for the selection of content area instructional materials that will support rather than frustrate student learning through reading. The five criteria are readability, concept load, background information, organization, and format and style. Each of these criteria will be considered in turn, and its application will be demonstrated through an analysis of *Man in the Tropics* (Carswell, Morrow and Honeybone, 1968), a textbook used in eighth grade social studies in British Columbia.

Readability

Readability as determined through readability formulas is often the first criterion used to select instructional materials. In 1963, Klare noted that over thirty different readability formulas existed. Since that time, a number of new formulas have been developed, including the relatively simple Fry (1968) and SMOG (McLaughlin, 1969) formulas. Most readability formulas use different combinations of sentence length and vocabulary difficulty to determine reading difficulty, while others include sentence complexity in their calculations.

Adapted from *Journal of Reading*, November 1977, *21*, 126-130.

But readability formulas can prove disillusioning. Often reading materials determined to be at the same level of reading difficulty cause students different degrees of reading difficulty in the classroom. Also, when different formulas are applied to the same material, they often yield different readability levels. Further confusion arises when students find materials with relatively low readability levels to be more difficult than expected, and the reverse.

The reasons for these anomalies lie in the nature of readability formulas themselves. Since methods for determining vocabulary difficulty and sentence length vary among formulas, as do the mathematical calculations used, the lack of consistency among the reading levels derived from different formulas is not surprising. And since formulas do not account for the complexity of ideas contained in reading materials, instances of "easy" materials proving difficult are understandable, since unfamiliar, complex concepts can be expressed using elementary vocabulary and short, simple sentences.

Readability formulas do provide a relatively quick guide to reading difficulty if their shortcomings are recognized and they are used together with other criteria. For example, *Man in the Tropics* checks out a grade nine reading level using the Fry formula but at a grade twelve level using the SMOG formula. About the only conclusion the teacher can draw from this information is that this material may be too difficult for most eighth graders. (The teacher may also be quietly thankful he is not teaching grades nine, ten, eleven, or twelve, in which case he would not know which formula to believe, or whether to believe either of them!)

Concept Load

According to Piaget (1971), it is only as students enter the period of formal operations from about age eleven onward that their conceptual development has advanced to the stage where they can internally build and manipulate abstract ideas without reference to concrete examples. This suggests that secondary students have only recently acquired the ability to comprehend abstract concepts, and that the nature and number of concepts introduced in content materials must be recognized as a major determiner of reading difficulty.

Concept load can be estimated by establishing the number of concepts introduced and their degree of complexity and level of abstraction. An examination of *Man in the Tropics* reveals that this book is likely to prove conceptually difficult for most eighth graders. The content of the book is beyond most students' direct experience. Moreover, students encounter a virtual avalanche of abstract concepts relating to geology, vegetation, climate, population, and agriculture, each concept being described by new technical vocabulary. This evidence supports the conclusion drawn from readability formulas that this book is going to be heavy going for most students in grade eight social studies.

Background Information

Since background information contributes directly to concept development, students' background information is closely related to concept load in determining the reading difficulty of instructional materials.

The teacher's first task is to determine the author's assumptions about students' background information and their previous learning experiences. Are these assumptions consistent with the background that students can be expected to bring to the new learning tasks? If these assumptions are not consistent, students will lack a context for new learning and comprehension difficulties will result.

Searching for the authors' assumptions about students' background information pertaining to the content of *Man in the Tropics* proves to be a futile exercise. Aside from a passing reference in the preface to "the range of ability of the students who will use this book," the authors make no direct reference to the students for whom their text is intended. One can only infer from the heavy concept load imposed by the content of their text that the authors assume considerable background information on the part of the reader.

The extent to which students will in fact possess this information can best be determined by the teacher. The importance of the teacher's role in deciding the appropriateness of instructional materials is highlighted here. In the case of *Man in the Tropics*, the eighth grade social studies teacher who is familiar with the social studies curriculum will be in the best position to determine what background information she can legitimately expect students to bring to this text based on their previous school experience.

Organization

Assuming that instructional materials present concepts consistent with students' backgrounds, one must also consider whether these concepts are organized to guide learning.

The teacher should check whether the internal organization of instructional materials provides a smooth continuity of ideas. Are concepts developed sequentially? Does one idea lead logically to the next? The provision of valid content alone does not ensure that this content will be organized in a clear and logical manner which is apparent to the reader.

Turning to *Man in the Tropics,* one finds a poorly organized text. While rich in content area information, the organization of this information fails to guide the development of students' geographic concepts. Rather than organizing their text around geographical concepts and developing these sequentially in order of their complexity and difficulty, the authors have chosen to organize their text around the different geographical regions studied. The result is that the stage of conceptual development and the amount of background information assumed to be possessed by students reading the first chapter are essentially the same as what are assumed in the final chapter; no development in learning through reading is provided for.

Format and Style

The format and style of instructional materials are also key considerations in determining reading difficulty. Obviously, students will read attractively laid out, colorful, and well illustrated instructional material in a more purposive manner and with greater success than they will "textbookish" material which promises little more than boredom.

Equally important is the author's style. Is the material written in a ponderous, overly academic style, or does the author project an empathy for the reading and learning tasks confronting students by writing in a manner which engages their attention and guides their thinking? No dilution of content or conceptual rigor need result from instructional materials written in approachable and appealing styles.

A further consideration is the provision of special features to aid learning. Graphic aids, illustrations, maps, glossaries, and appendices all assist student learning when they are well integrated with the text of the material. The specific nature of these aids will vary widely from one content area to another. In assessing the effectiveness of these aids, the teacher should check that they are located where they are needed within the material, and not relegated to the back of the book or placed several pages away from their optimally useful location in the text.

The format and style of *Man in the Tropics* are adequate but not outstanding. There are ample illustrations, and the text is written directly to the student, thereby giving the student a sense of active involvement with the material. Special features abound in the text, but a careful examination of them reveals flaws in their placement and content. For example, the first paragraph of the first chapter refers the student to a figure which does not appear until three pages later, and further on in the text the student is directed to compare the features of two racial groups in a series of photographs, only to find just one of the groups represented!

The five criteria for materials selection outlined here are suggestive, not prescriptive. Additional or different criteria may be indicated in specific learning situations and in particular content areas. However, the application of these five criteria will give a general framework for selecting instructional materials which support student learning of content through reading.

Should the grade eight social studies teacher adopt *Man in the Tropics?* Ultimately, the decision must be based on knowledge of the students. But the evidence revealed by the analysis illustrated here strongly suggests that this text will make difficult reading for most eighth graders. Readability, concept load, assumed background information, organization, and certain aspects of format all contribute to a difficult text. Significantly, no one category of information is sufficient to classify accurately this text. But taken together, the information from the various categories presents a composite picture of a piece of instructional material which may be all too typical in its inadequate recognition of the learning needs of the students for whom it is intended.

References

Carswell, Gordon E., Robert Morrow and R.C. Honeybone. *Man in the Tropics.* Toronto, Ont.: Bellhaven House, 1968.

Fry, Edward. "A Readability Formula that Saves Time." *Journal of Reading,* vol. 11, no. 7 (April 1968), pp. 513-16.

Klare, George R. *The Measurement of Readability.* Ames, Iowa: Iowa State University Press, 1963.

McLaughlin, Harry G. "SMOG Grading—A New Readability Formula." *Journal of Reading,* vol. 12, no. 8 (May 1969), pp. 639-46.

Piaget, Jean. *Science of Education and the Psychology of the Child.* New York, N.Y.: Viking Press, 1971.

● *First, read figure 2 in the article.*
● *Then, read the article itself to see how Fry deals with each issue he raises concerning the measurement of readability.*

FRY'S READABILITY GRAPH: CLARIFICATIONS, VALIDITY, AND EXTENSION TO LEVEL 17

Edward Fry
Rutgers University

I find myself in the somewhat untenable position of having several books in print (Fry, 1963, 1972, 1977) that give differing instructions regarding the inclusion of proper nouns when using the Fry readability graph. The latest book, a version of the graph in slide rule form (Fry, 1976), suggests that proper nouns should be included in the word count, and this article will discuss briefly the reasons for including them. In addition, I would like to take up some other areas related to readability estimates and the use of my graph. Specifically, a number of questions have been presented to me regarding somewhat detailed but very real problems such as what a syllable is and what a word is—for example, is *stopped* a two syllable word, and is *1945* or *IRA* a word? A third area concerns the problems of validity and reliability of readability scores, and recent work being done on new ways to establish this. Finally, an extension of my graph upward into the college levels will be presented.

I must confess that when I first developed the readability graph in Africa in about 1961, I had no idea that anyone would take it very seriously, or that so many thousands of people would start using it. If I had, I might have put more care into its development, but on the other hand, if it was to be a large research project with a proper statistical design, it might have never seen the light of day. Its original purpose, and its present purpose, is to aid teachers and editors to help children or adults read better by giving them material on the proper difficulty level.

At the time of the graph's origin, I had a Fulbright lectureship at Makerere College in Uganda, and my purpose was to help a group of African

Adapted from *Journal of Reading*, December 1977, *21*, 242-252.

teachers on a UNESCO training project who were teaching English as a second language. It was first published in a British journal (1964) and as an appendix in my book, *Teaching Faster Reading* (1963), which was also originally written for those same UNESCO teachers. As near as I know, for years nobody ever used the graph; it was not reprinted or cited, nor did I get any informal feedback about usage. From this, I can possibly conclude that American educators do not read British journals, or that its essentially British designations (1000 word level, 2000 word level, etc., and the Oxford English Readers series book levels) were too parochial. It might also be that readability was not a terribly popular topic in the early 1960s; certainly it doesn't use up much space in teacher training books of that period.

However, under the principle of "never throw out your old good ideas, just dust them off occasionally and see if they will fly," I started doing a bit more with readability in teacher training. Next, I added some Americanization (grade levels) and validation of the graph at the secondary level (Fry, 1968) and the primary level (Fry, 1969). It was after the appearance of these two articles that American educators began to use the graph, first in teacher training classes, then in textbooks.

Certainly, readability had been around for a number of years, possibly formally beginning with Lively and Pressey in 1923, but few people outside of reading specialists and researchers used it. Then readability began getting great surges of momentum from other formula builders, such as Lorge in 1939, Flesch in 1943, Dale and Chall in 1948, and Spache in 1953. When teachers began asking publishers about the readability of their books, the publishers began to take a greater interest in readability.

The Readability Graph's contribution seems to be in simplicity of use without sacrificing much, if any, accuracy, and its wide and continuous range from grade one up through college. That it was not copyrighted and could be reproduced on one sheet of paper might have helped also.

Surprisingly, few people ask me what the curved line in the graph represents (it has little to do with the graph's use). Not deterred by this lack of curiosity, I will tell you anyway. It is the smoothed mean of the plots of sample passages. If you plot a large number of passages with a wide range, they will tend to fall somewhere near the line. In short, it is an "eyeball" job. However, my friends in higher mathematics tell me that "smoothing a curve" in this manner is just about as accurate as doing it by complicated formula.

The grade areas were assigned the same way, only this time the grade level for each plot was necessary to delineate concentrations. The grade lines were made perpendicular to the curved line (which is one reason the curve was made in the first place), and they were adjusted a little when correlation studies were done with more material and other formulas, such as the Spache and the Dale-Chall. It is of moderate consternation that the grade level areas came out unequal size, but I chose to follow the old researcher's maxim: "When in doubt, believe the data."

Fortunately, time and other research studies have continued to show the efficacy of the two inputs of the graph, syllables and sentence length. Klare (1974-1975), a widely recognized bibliographer of readability studies, has summarized:

> Unless the user is interested in doing research, there is little to be gained from choosing a highly complex formula. A simple 2-variable formula should be sufficient, especially if one of the variables is a word or semantic variable and the other is a sentence or syntactic variable...If the count is to be made by hand, counting syllables in some fashion...is somewhat faster than using most word lists.

Zipf's principle—that higher frequency words are shorter— seems intact (1965).

Include Proper Nouns

It is always embarrassing to admit mistakes, especially if they are in print and thousands of people know about them, but I think I made a mistake in the 1968 article in which I included the sentence in the graph directions, "Don't count proper nouns." The first two publications of the graph (1963 and 1964) said nothing about omitting proper nouns. Somehow or other, possibly because of influence of other formulas which had specific instructions about not counting proper nouns, I omitted them in 1968. I would like to reverse this decision now and say that they should be included.

The reasons for doing this are simultaneously subjective, logical, and empirical. Proper nouns do contribute to the difficulty of the material. It is easier for a child to read "Joe" than "Joseph," and children or adults certainly do not skip proper nouns in most reading. Complaints about using proper nouns do not come from teachers, but most often from editors of texts who have difficulty in getting the readability low enough for the grade level at which they hope to sell the book.

Empirically, both the 1968 article and a recent thesis by Zingman (1977) show that the grade level designations of the graph are a little on the low side, compared with other formulas (about a year, in many instances), when the graph is used without proper nouns.

A recent study by Britton and Lumpkin (1977) using a large number of samples and comparing the Fry formula (with proper nouns) and five other formulas plus publisher designations, also tends to support the inclusion of proper nouns. The data in the table show almost perfect agreement in ranking and close agreement in grade level designations.

Britton and Lumpkin, incidentally, used my formula slightly differently from the published directions; they averaged a large number of grade level designations and thus obtained grade level designations with a decimal point. The regular directions call for the averaging of the syllables and sentence length, *then* entering the graph to get a whole grade level designation. I do not find their procedure objectionable since they did it with a large number of samples (on a computer). However, users must continually be aware that readability scores are estimates and the individual samples jump around a mean score, as was demonstrated by Coke and Rothkopf (1970) (see figure).

A Comparison of Publishers' Designations with Six Readability Formulas for the Ginn Reading 720 Series (1976)

Publisher's Book Level	No. of 100 word samples	Fry[a] $(1-3)$[b]	Harris-Jacobson $(PP - 8+)$[b]	Readability Spache $(1-3)$[b]	Dale-Chall $(4-16)$[b]	Flesch $(5-17)$[b]	Farr-Jenkins-Patterson $(5-17)$[b]
Preprimer	8	1.0	.5	1.3			
Primer	8	1.0	1.0	1.6			
1	23	1.1	1.2	1.7			
2_1	26	2.2	1.8	1.9			
2_2	26	2.7	2.5	2.3			
3_1	26	2.7	2.6	2.5			
3_2	20	4.0	3.1	2.7			
4_1	28	4.2	3.7		5.3		
4_2	29	4.4	3.8		5.3		
5	26	5.8	5.3		6.7	6.8	8.7
6	37	6.6	5.6		7.5	7.2	8.9

Source: Abstracted from *A Consumer's Guide on Readability* by Gwyneth Britton and Margaret Lumpkin. G. Britton and Associates, Corvallis, Oregon, 1977.

[a] The Fry word and syllable count uses proper nouns.

[b] The numbers in parentheses are the range of the formula in grade levels. This also explains why all formulas are not used at all levels.

By including proper nouns in the count, if we err, we err on the side of the angels, or perhaps you might say on the side of the children, if you perceive the two not to be synonymous. Causing the teacher to select easier books for the child to read will do nothing but increase the child's comprehension, pleasure, and inclination to keep reading.

Syllables and Words

Graph users sometimes have a little bit of trouble in determining syllables. Much of this is caused by a dissonance between phonetic and graphic considerations. To illustrate, *wanted* is a two-syllable word but *stopped* is one syllable. The quick answer is, believe what you hear, not what you see. In other words, when counting syllables, go by speech sounds. Fortunately, most people, including children, can fairly accurately determine the number of phonetic syllables in a passage. Children don't have any trouble syllabifying *Sall-y-is-a-scard-y-cat.*

The problem comes with literate teachers who know that many affixes form separate syllables. They do have a leg to stand upon, because morphology influences syllabification, but an overriding principle is that every syllable has a separate vowel sound.

In most prose counts, there is no problem in defining what a word is, but for those graph users who request a more precise statement, I suggest the computer definition: A word is a symbol or group of symbols bounded by a blank space on either side. Thus, *1945, &,* and *IRA* are all words.

A problem now arises as to how many syllables you allot for these strange words. In an effort to keep it simple but logical, I suggest that each symbol receive a syllable count of one. Thus, *1945* is four syllables, *&* is one, and *IRA* is three.

In the case of initialisms like *IRA*, where each letter is spoken, the rule follows the general phonetic syllable principle, and *US* is easier to read than *USOE.* Numbers are similar — there is surface validity to the idea that 43,172 is harder to read than 72, which is harder to read than 2. This suggestion might aid those who tackle the difficult problem of readability of mathematics texts.

Incidentally, I have been asked many times about how to use readability formulas on mathematics textbooks. There is no simple answer. Readability formulas were made for prose, not numerical formulas or poetry. The new policy stated above will help in the prose parts of the math text, but the parts that have many numbers or mathematical formulas must rely on another type of difficulty evaluation. I suggest that there is no substitute for trying out the passage or book on a sample population for whom the book is intended.

Reliability and Validity

A readability formula is in many respects like a reading test, except instead of testing children, it tests written material. Hence, it is proper to assume that many testing concepts should apply. Readability formulas are not strong in reporting either reliability or validity.

We can assume that the formulas have at least a modest amount of reliability because they consistently correlate fairly well with each other, but direct measures and useful statistics like Standard Error of Measurement are usually not given. As a notable exception, Spache (1966) reported a probable error of 3.3 months.

When trying to find the reliability of a formula, we encounter the problem that written prose samples contain a good deal of variability. When Coke and Rothkopf (1970) programmed a computer to continuously sample every hundred words for a 20,000 word passage, they found that the readability scores tended to follow a normal distribution curve. We could expect that writers have different amounts of variability or consistency in writing on grade level; hence, if unreliability is found, it could be the formula, or it could be the variability in writing.

Figure 1

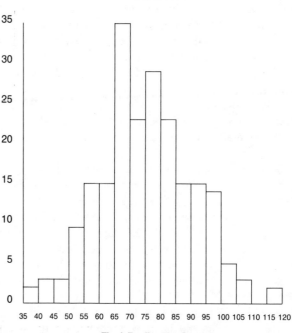

Flesch Reading Ease Score

This graph shows an approximately normal distribution of readability difficulty levels when 200 continuous 100-word samples were rated for readability using the Flesch Reading Ease Scores on a passage about modern physics. It illustrates why it is necessary to take multiple samples from a passage in order to arrive at a true mean score. Graph taken from Coke and Rothkopf (1970).

Validity of formulas is approached in a number of different ways, such as correlations between formulas or correlations with comprehension scores, with cloze scores, with oral reading errors, with observer judgment, and with written passages of known difficulty. My graph has been validated by interformula and comprehension scores (Fry, 1968) and oral reading errors (Fry, 1969; Paolo, 1977). Indirectly, it is validated by studies such as Zingman's (1977) and those by Dulin (1969), who did readability on a number of national news stories, and by Britton and Lumpkin (1977), who found that the graph produced scores similar to those from other formulas (see table).

Another method of estimating readability is by using judges. Developing the SEER (Singer Eyeball Estimate of Readability), Singer (1975) had thirty-two college students judge eight paragraphs ranging from grades one to seven. He concluded, "Results revealed the average discrepancy in readability levels established by the SEER technique and those computed by readability formulas (Spache and Dale-Chall) was less than one grade level. Moreover, the SEER technique was as valid as the Fry graphed procedure, but took much less time, an average of only two minutes per paragraph." I might point out that if you wish to save all this time and get the same degree of validity reported by Singer, you have to have thirty-two judges working for two minutes, then average their findings.

Carver (1975-1976) also compared the graph with his Rauding technique, which used trained judges for comparing prose samples against a standard. He also compared the graph with cloze rankings (Bormuth levels). The graph correlated .85 with Rauding technique and .81 with Bormuth level. Incidentally, it correlated .95 with Flesch and .85 with Dale-Chall.

However, both Singer and Carver have demonstrated that it is possible to judge the difficulty levels of unknown writing samples subjectively, and this can be seen as a contribution to the validity of readability formulas.

It might also be noted that Singer, and many others, use the graph in a manner contrary to directions, namely, they take the estimated grade level based on only one sample. The directions state that three or more samples should be averaged. The graph will yield a grade level score for a 100 word sample, but the user should be aware that there is necessarily a sacrifice in both reliability and validity.

A very interesting validation of readability formulas has been done in journalistic studies. I am mentioning it here, not because it is new but because it is in literature not always searched by reading researchers. Journalists tend to use such techniques as split runs, in which half the papers carry an article written at one grade level and half carry it written at a lower grade level. They then sample the readership utilizing such dependent variables as amount of people reading the story and number of paragraphs read. Writing to lower readability often substantially increases readership (Lyman, 1949; Murphy, 1947; Swanson, 1948).

Researchers are continually looking for new methods of validating readability formulas. Ernest Rothkopf at Bell Laboratories is currently experimenting with something called "functional chaining." In simplified terms, a functional chain is the number of words a typist can continue typing after the copy has been removed from site. This was found to be related to the Flesch reading case index, syntactic complexity, familiarity with topical content, and eye movement patterns during learning. This is similar to the work of Holgerson (1977) who compared eye-voice span on passages of differing difficulty and with readers at different levels.

Hardyck and Petrinovich (1970) found that when students are asked to read easy and hard passages silently while sensitive measures of muscle activity in the oral area are recorded, subvocalization increases as reading difficulty of material increases. In an extension of this work at the Rutgers Reading Center, Leo Campbell is using myographs to record oral muscle activity during reading of passages that increase in syntactic difficulty and of passages that increase in vocabulary difficulty.

In summary, readability formulas can be validated by a wide variety of measures, and their reliability is attested to by intercorrelations. However, this does not mean that there is not plenty of work left to do in the way of refinements as well as basic understandings.

Graph Modifications

Several investigators have attempted to refine my readability graph. Maginnis (1969) extended the graph downward into the preprimer levels and used it with shorter passages. Considering the general lack of pinpoint reliability of formulas, this distinction within grade levels is not warranted. I have no reason to think that my graph is any more accurate than Spache's, for example, and he only knows where a book is within .6 of a year and 50 percent of the time. Also, on a logical level, a beginning reader is so dependent on the particular basal series that he has used in the first half of the year that there seems to be little benefit in determining a generalized readability for that level. Kretschmer (1976), on the other hand, tried to improve the accuracy of the graph by adding a set of vocabulary words to be consulted. This tends to complicate the graph's use, and unless he or somebody can demonstrate that there is a significant improvement in accuracy, we should hold this modification in abeyance.

GRAPH FOR ESTIMATING READABILITY – EXTENDED

by Edward Fry, Rutgers University Reading Center, New Brunswick, N.J. 08904

Average number of syllables per 100 words

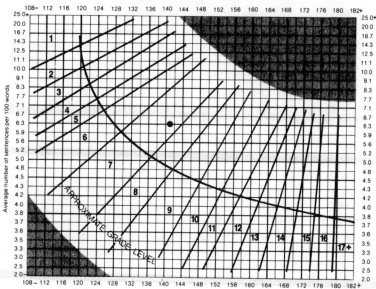

Expanded Directions for Working Readability Graph

1. Randomly select three (3) sample passages and count out exactly 100 words each, beginning with the beginning of a sentence. Do count proper nouns, initializations, and numerals.
2. Count the number of sentences in the hundred words, estimating length of the fraction of the last sentence to the nearest one-tenth.
3. Count the total number of syllables in the 100-word passage. If you don't have a hand counter available, an easy way is to simply put a mark above every syllable over one in each word, then when you get to the end of the passage, count the number of marks and add 100. Small calculators can also be used as counters by pushing numeral 1, then push the + sign for each word or syllable when counting.
4. Enter graph with *average* sentence length and *average* number of syllables; plot dot where the two lines intersect. Area where dot is plotted will give you the approximate grade level.
5. If a great deal of variability is found in syllable count or sentence count, putting more samples into the average is desirable.
6. A word is defined as a group of symbols with a space on either side; thus, *Joe, IRA, 1945,* and & are each one word.
7. A syllable is defined as a phonetic syllable. Generally, there are as many syllables as vowel sounds. For example, *stopped* is one syllable and *wanted* is two syllables. When counting syllables for numerals and initializations, count one syllable for each symbol. For example, *1945* is four syllables, *IRA* is three syllables, and & is one syllable.

Note: This "extended graph" does not outmode or render the earlier (1968) version inoperative or inaccurate; it is an extension. (REPRODUCTION PERMITTED—NO COPYRIGHT)

Fry

There have been numerous attempts to improve readability determination through studying syntax variations. Two of these have been closely related to the graph and some work that I have done. At the twenty-fourth annual meeting of the National Reading Conference, I proposed the Kernel Distance Theory, which tried to explain why two sentences containing essentially equal words, hence equal length and equal syllables and the same or nearly the same meaning, can have unequal difficulty (Fry, 1975a). For example:

> No belief, if injustices and evils are to be eradicated, can be regarded as infallible.
> No belief can be regarded as infallible if injustices and evils are to be eradicated.

The Kernel Distance Theory defines the kernel of a sentence as the noun (subject), verb (predicate), and sometimes an object. Distance applies to any word or phrase not a part of the kernel. The theory then states that distance between the noun and the verb makes the sentence harder then does distance outside the kernel, as in the example above.

This part of the theory was confirmed in a dissertation by DePierro (1976), who presented pairs of sentences to fifth and sixth graders and to college undergraduates and asked them to recall the sentences; he also noted their silent reading time and response time after presentation. It was also confirmed in a master's thesis by Weber (1977), who used subjective judgment of junior college students.

Two other parts of the theory were not confirmed: that distance before the kernel caused more difficulty than distance after the kernel, and that distance between noun and verb caused more difficulty than distance between verb and object.

This research has more implication for writers than for construction of readability formulas. It suggests that one way writers can lower readability levels is to avoid splitting the kernel of a sentence; however, this will not affect the readability score on most formulas.

Another way of looking at grammatical complexity was investigated by Pearson (1974-1975), who pointed out that in some specific instances, longer sentences produced better comprehension than short sentences. For example, when two short sentences were put together and a "because" was added, questions about the relationship between the sentences were easier. Pearson is undoubtedly correct in specific instances, as in the Kernel Distance Theory in the noun-verb split for instance, but these specific conditions are statistically not common, and I believe that Klare's general statement about sentence length increasing difficulty still holds for general use.

Graph Extension

With considerable trepidation, I have extended the graph through the college years by simple extrapolation. The college year areas are based on the average areas for the preceding three years. It is known that vocabulary continues to increase throughout the college years; however, I openly confess to not having any data about the difference between thirteenth through sixteenth grade material. I do hope someone will gather some for validation.

In the meantime, I have had requests for some kind of objective measurement of material difficulty in the college areas. I am, therefore, proposing this extension as a relative difficulty differentiation rather than a normed score. In other words, I believe that it is somewhat defensible to state that a book scoring at level sixteen is more difficult than a book scoring at level fourteen, but it is not appropriate to say that one is suitable for college seniors and the other for college sophomores.

Part of the difficulty in determining college norms is that college populations have wide divergences in academic qualifications of students. College reading ability also tends to become very "subject specific." That means that what may be normal reading for a physics student could be quite difficult for a philosophy student and vice versa. These variables are all in addition to the readability principle that "High motivation overcomes high readability level, but low motivation demands a low readability level" (Fry, 1975b).

This article is intended to update readers on some background and some activity in the area of readability with particular reference to my readability graph. Readability continues to be an active area of research and fortunately an actively used tool for practicing teachers and curriculum material developers. I hope that some of the new rules on word count and the extension to college level material will prove helpful and that some of the discussion of recent research will stimulate others to work in this interesting area of the reading field.

References

Bormuth, John R. "Readability: A New Approach." *Reading Research Quarterly,* vol. 1 (Fall 1966), pp. 79-132.

Britton, Gwyneth and Margaret Lumpkin. *A Consumer's Guide on Readability: Ginn and Company, Ginn Reading 720, 1976.* Corvallis, Ore.: G. Britton and Associates, 1977.

Carver, Ronald P. "Measuring Prose Difficulty Using the Rauding Scale." *Reading Research Quarterly,* vol. 11, no. 4 (1975-1976), pp. 660-85.

Coke, Esther U. and Ernst Z. Rothkopf. "Note on a Simple Algorithm for a Computer Produced Reading Ease Score. *Journal of Applied Psychology,* vol. 54 (1970), pp. 208-10.

Dale, Edgar and Jeanne Chall. "A Formula for Predicting Readability." *Educational Research Bulletin,* vol. 27 (January 1948), pp. 11-20.

DePierro, Joseph. Some Effects of Sentence Structure Variables on Reading Ease. Unpublished doctoral dissertation. Rutgers University, New Brunswick, N.J., June 1976.

Dulin, K. "Readability Levels of Adult Magazine Material." *The Psychology of Reading Behavior,* George Schick and Merrill May, Eds., pp. 176-80. 18th Yearbook, National Reading Conference, Clemson University, Clemson, S.C. 1969.

Flesch, Rudolf F. "A New Readability Yardstick." *Journal of Applied Psychology,* vol. 32 (June 1948), pp. 221-33.

Flesch, Rudolf F. *Marks of Readable Style: A Study in Adult Education.* New York, N.Y.: Bureau of Publications, Teachers College, Columbia University, 1943.

Fry, Edward B. *Teaching Faster Reading.* London: Cambridge University Press, 1963.

Fry, Edward B. "A Readability Estimate Graph for Any English Language Material." *Teacher Education.* London: Oxford University Press, May 1964.

Fry, Edward B. "A Readability Formula that Saves Time." *Journal of Reading,* vol. 11, no. 7 (April 1968), pp. 513-16, 575-78.

Fry, Edward B. "The Readability Graph Validated at Primary Levels." *The Reading Teacher,* vol. 22, no. 6 (March 1969), pp. 534-38.

Fry, Edward B. *Reading Instruction for Classroom and Clinic.* New York, N.Y.: McGraw-Hill, 1972.

Fry, Edward B. "A Kernel Distance Theory for Readability." *Reading Convention and Inquiry,* George McNinch and Wallace D. Miller, Eds. 24th Yearbook, National Reading Conference, Clemson University, Clemson, S.C., 1975a.

Fry, Edward B. "The Readability Principle." *Language Arts,* vol. 52, no. 6 (September 1975b), pp. 847-51.

Fry, Edward B. *Fry Readability Scale.* Providence, R.I.: Jamestown Publishers, 1976.

Fry, Edward B. *Elementary Reading Instruction.* New York, N.Y.: McGraw-Hill, 1977.

Hardyck, C.D. and L.F. Petrinovich. "Subvocal Speech and Comprehension Level as a Function of the Difficulty Level of Reading Material." *Journal of Verbal Learning and Verbal Behavior,* vol. 9 (1970), pp. 647-52.

Holgerson, Arnold S. The Relationship of Eye-Voice Span to Reading Ability and Readability. Unpublished master's thesis, Rutgers University, New Brunswick, N.J., June 1977. (Available through ERIC.)

Klare, George R. "Assessing Readability." *Reading Research Quarterly,* vol. 10, no. 1 (1974-1975), pp. 62-102.

Kretschmer, Joseph C. "Updating the Fry Readability Formula." *The Reading Teacher,* vol. 29, no. 6 (March 1976), pp. 555-58.

Lively, Bertha A. and S. L. Pressey. "A Method for Measuring the 'Vocabulary Burden' of Text Books." *Educational Administration and Supervision,* vol. 9 (Oct. 1923), pp. 389-98.

Lorge, Irving I. *The Lorge Formula for Estimating Difficulty of Reading Materials.* New York, N.Y.: Bureau of Publications, Teachers College, Columbia University, 1959.

Lorge, Irving I. "Predicting Reading Difficulty of Selections for Children." *The Elementary English Review,* vol. 16 (October 1939), pp. 229-33.

Lyman, H. "Flesch Count and the Readership of Articles in a Midwestern Farm Paper." *Journal of Applied Psychology,* vol. 33 (1949), pp. 78-80.

Maginnis, George H. "The Readability Graph and Informal Reading Inventories." *The Reading Teacher,* vol. 22, no. 6 (March 1969), pp. 516-18, 559.

Murphy, D. "Test Proves Short Words and Sentences Get Best Readership." *Printer's Ink,* no. 218 (January 10, 1947), pp. 61-64.

Murphy, D. "How Plain Talk Increases Readership 45% to 66%." *Printer's Ink,* no. 220 (September 19, 1947), pp. 35-37.

Paolo, Margaret F. A Comparison of Readability Graph Scores and Oral Reading Errors on Trade Books for Beginning Reading. Unpublished master's thesis. Rutgers University, New Brunswick, N.J., January 1977. (Available through ERIC.)

Pearson, David P. "The Effects of Grammatical Complexity on Children's Comprehension, Recall, and Conceptions of Certain Semantic Relations." *Reading Research Quarterly,* vol. 10, no. 2 (1974-1975), pp. 155-92.

Rothkopf, Ernst Z. "Text Difficulty Predicted from Functional Chaining in Short Term Memory." *Abstracts of Papers and Symposia.* Annual Meeting, American Educational Research Association, 1977.

Singer, Harry. "The SEER Technique: A Non-Computational Procedure for Quickly Estimating Readability Level." *Journal of Reading Behavior,* vol. 7, no. 3 (1975), pp. 255-67.

Spache, George. "A New Readability Formula for Primary Grades Reading Materials." *Elementary English,* vol. 53 (March 1953), pp. 410-13.

Spache, George. *Good Books for Poor Readers.* Champaign, Ill.: Gerrard Publishing Co., 1966.

Swanson, C. "Readability and Readership: A Controlled Experiment." *Journalism Quarterly,* vol. 25 (1948), pp. 339-45.

Weber, Jane E. The Kernel Distance Theory—Evaluation by Student Judgment of Sentence Difficulty. Unpublished master's thesis. Rutgers University, New Brunswick, N.J., June 1977. (Available through ERIC.)

Zingman, Doris E. Readability and Mass Political Literature: The 1976 Presidential Election Campaign. Unpublished master's thesis. Rutgers University, New Brunswick, N.J., June 1977. (Available through ERIC.)

Zipf, G.K. *The Psycho-Biology of Language.* Boston: Houghton Mifflin, 1935. (Reprinted, Cambridge, Mass.: MIT Press, 1965.)

- *What two common uses of readability formulas does the author question?*
- *What specific suggestions are given for using readability formulas?*

READABILITY: SOME CAUTIONS FOR THE CONTENT AREA TEACHER

Joan Nelson-Herber
State University of New York at Binghamton

Professional textbooks that promote reading instruction in content areas typically recommend that classroom teachers use a readability formula to determine the appropriateness of subject area text materials for their students. Good advice? It depends.

Every teacher should be able to estimate the reading difficulty of materials that students are expected to read. Obviously, it is useful to have some objective means for making this estimate. The most widely used readability formulas (Dale-Chall 1948, Flesch 1951, Fry 1968, McLaughlin 1969) employ some measure of sentence length along with some measure of word difficulty to determine a grade level score for printed materials. The score is usually based on sample passages drawn from various parts of the text, and it represents an estimate of the average reading difficulty of the full text. Different formulas yield slightly different readability scores for a given selection, but teachers can use the score as one factor in evaluating reading material for student use.

Readability scores provide *estimates* of reading difficulty, not firm and absolute levels. Recommending the use of readability formulas is good advice if their limitations are communicated along with their recommendation. However, some suggestions of how to use the information derived from a formula call into question the appropriateness of recommending their use in the first place. Content area teachers are frequently advised to use readability scores to match the reading difficulty level of text materials to the reading achievement level of individual students. Occasionally, it is suggested that teachers should rewrite text materials to conform to read-

Adapted from *Journal of Reading,* April 1978, *21,* 620-625.

ability criteria. Based on both practical and theoretical considerations, these recommendations are questionable at best and may be harmful in practice unless caution prevails.

While it may make very good sense for a reading teacher to choose or prepare materials for reading instruction that approximate the reading achievement level of the individual student, a variety of factors make it impractical and perhaps even inadvisable for content area teachers to do the same. The curriculum for the reading teacher is the reading process, most often defined as a set of reading skills. The reading teacher analyzes specific skill needs of individual students and selects or prepares material that lends itself to the sequential development of needed skills.

The curriculum of the content area teacher, on the other hand, is a set of ideas and generalizations related to the subject of study (Herber 1970). For the subject area teacher, the most important consideration in selecting text material is whether it communicates the essential facts, concepts, and values of the subject in a logical sequence, a sensible organization, and an interesting and attractive format. Readability is an important factor, of course. It would be foolish to expect students to comprehend written material far above their reading level no matter how well it presented the essential information. However, given the wide range of reading achievement to be found in a typical class at the middle or secondary school level, it is unrealistic to expect subject area teachers to locate material containing the essentials of the subject for each level of reading achievement represented in the classroom.

According to Burmeister (1974) and others, the typical tenth grade classroom encompasses a range of eleven grades of reading achievement, from fourth grade to college level. Even if it were possible to approximate this range with several sets of material containing the essential information, it would be inappropriate to assume that students could comprehend any given text simply because readability scores matched reading achievement scores. Too many factors other than sentence length and word difficulty are involved in comprehending contact area material to make any such assumption.

Readability formulas do not generally consider such variables as levels of abstraction, complexity of concepts, figurative and poetic language, multiple meanings, technical and scientific vocabulary, variations in format and organization, and a host of other factors related to the comprehensibility of subject area reading materials [Some readability formulas do consider sentence complexity and, to some extent, concept load. They are, however, more complicated to calculate, and their use is generally confined to researchers. Klare (1974, 1975) provides an excellent summary of readability formulas for interested readers.] Neither do they take into account the variability of reading difficulty within text material except in the averaging process. More important, readability formulas do not measure the interest, the motivation, the language competence, or the experiential background of the reader in relation to the specific content of the text.

Take the following social studies sentences as an example: "The leader often becomes the symbol of the unity of the country. No one will run against him." These sentences are relatively short and they contain few multisyllabic words. According to readability criteria, the sentences would appear to be appropriate for junior high school text material. However, the difficulty an eighth grade reader might experience in comprehending these sentences has little to do with readability criteria. Consider the information that the student must integrate:

1. The special meaning of *leader* in the social studies context.
2. The word *often* used to mean "in many cases" rather than "repeatedly."
3. The sense of *becomes* as meaning "grows to be" rather than "is suitable to."
4. The abstract concept of symbolism.
5. The abstract concept of unity.
6. The word *country* as a political unit rather than as a rural area.
7. The idea of *run* against as in an election.
8. The implication of a cause and effect relationship between the ideas presented in the two sentences.

There is no question that the context of the full text would support the idea being presented. Unfortunately the surrounding sentences are likely to contain other abstractions, multiple meaning words, and implied relationships that pose their own comprehension problems.

It is clear, then, that the danger is not in advising teachers to use readability formulas as an aid in evaluating student textbooks; the danger is in promoting the faulty assumption that matching the readability score of materials to the reading achievement scores of students will automatically yield comprehension. Far too many teachers make textbook reading assignments on the basis of that faulty assumption and then fail to comprehend why students fail to comprehend.

Rewriting Text Materials

Recommendations that teachers rewrite text materials to meet readability criteria are based on another faulty assumption—that shortening sentences and changing multisyllabic words automatically make a reading passage easier. According to Pearson (1974-1975, p. 160), "Such recommendations reveal a common error in interpreting correlational data by assuming that correlation means causality."

Readability formulas are based on correlational data. Correlation is simply an index of relationship. Although sentence length correlates with passage reading difficulty, it is not necessarily the cause of the reading difficulty. It may be that concept complexity causes both longer sentences *and* reading difficulty. Clear communication of complex concepts may *require* longer sentences. Thus, the reading difficulty of a passage would be caused by complex concept load which results in a longer sentence, rather than by sentence length itself. Shortening the sentence without changing the concept load may not enhance comprehension. Indeed, there is a growing body of evidence and opinion (Pearson 1974-1975, Dawkins 1975, Klare 1974-1975) to suggest that arbitrarily shortening sentences may *increase* the difficulty of the reading task by rendering explicit relationships obscure.

Pearson uses the following example:
    (a) Because the chain broke, the machine stopped.
    (b) The chain broke. The machine stopped.

Though sentence (a) is longer, the causal relationship is made explicit by the subordinating conjunction. In (b) we have reduced the sentence length but have placed a new inferential burden on the reader. The causal relationship must be inferred 1) from the proximity of the ideas presented and 2) from the reader's background of experience with machines.

The increase in difficulty may not be apparent here, because most people have had some experience with machines; however, where subject area textbooks are presenting ideas that are *new* to the reader, that is *beyond the reader's experience,* such causal relationships might be impossible to infer, as in the following sentences which might be found in an economics textbook: "Businessmen are forced to lower investment. They change their production and employment levels to return to equilibrium." Does a cause and effect relationship exist between the two sentences? If so, which is cause and which is effect? Unless the reader is familiar with the economic principles of income determination, it is impossible to be sure. Compare the longer sentence: "*Because* businessmen are forced to lower investment, they change their production and employment levels to return to equilibrium." The relationship is made explicit, leaving the reader free to ponder the meanings of the words themselves.

What about the words themselves? According to Klare (1974-1975, p. 96), "the word or semantic variable is consistently more highly predictive than the sentence or syntactic variable when each is considered singly." It might seem to make sense, then, to change difficult or multisyllabic words to meet readability criteria. Unfortunately, the words that are most likely to cause a high readability score for a content area textbook are the technical vocabulary and the special meaning words of the subject area. For example: in mathematics — multiplication, rectangular, hypotenuse, variables, adjacent, circumference, congruent; in social studies — peninsula, totalitarianism, historical, equilibrium, vegetation, distribution, discrimination, industrialization, reciprocity; in science — elements, chemicals, reaction, reagent, acceleration, condensation, chromosomes, photosynthesis, precipitation.

These are only samples of the kinds of content words which are either multisyllabic or do not appear on lists of commonly used words such as the Dale-Chall list (1948). They are, nevertheless, essential to subject matter comprehension. It would be foolish to suggest that teachers rewrite materials to change or eliminate these words when they represent the very substance of the subject the teachers are trying to teach.

To return to our earlier economics example, the words *businessmen, investment, production, employment,*and *equilibrium* are those which most readability criteria would suggest changing for reading ease. However, these words represent the technical vocabulary of the subject. Without an understanding of these words, students would be crippled in their study of economics. These words should be taught, not changed or eliminated. Thus, instruction, not a readability formula, becomes the key to comprehension of subject area material.

A content area textbook is not really designed for independent reading. It is a teaching tool designed to present facts, concepts, and values that are beyond the current knowledge and experience of the reader. The textbook uses the technical vocabulary of the subject to convey that information. Imbedded within that text are abstractions, comparisons and contrasts, cause and effect relationships, and sequences of events related to the subject. The use of a formula based on word difficulty and sentence length to match the readability score of material to reading achievement score of the reader does not automatically yield reading comprehension. Comprehension of the text requires the integration of what is new to the reader with his or her own background of experience. The reader makes sense of what is unfamiliar by relating it with the familiar.

The essence of good teaching is showing the learner how to do what is required to be successful (Herber 1970). The teacher provides the link between the familiar and the unfamiliar through instruction. The more experience the reader has had with the vocabulary and concepts of the subject, the easier the textbook will be to read and comprehend. Instruction in content area reading includes:

1. Putting students in touch with their own experience that relates to the new ideas being studied.

2. Teaching vocabulary in a way that relates the new words to previous experience to give the learner a context for meaning.

3. Guiding reading to provide the support needed to understand new ideas by setting purposes for reading; calling attention to organization; preparing material to demonstrate relationships such as cause-effect, comparison-contrast, and sequences; and preparing material to aid students in reading for information, interpretation, and application.

4. Providing post-reading activities to encourage rereading, discussion, and reinforcement of the new ideas in the context of the student's own world of experience.

Teaching strategies to accomplish such reading instruction in content areas have been amply described and demonstrated in Herber (1970, 1978), Robinson (1975), Shepherd (1973), Herber and Nelson (1977), and others.

Suggestions for Content Teachers

The preceding ideas can be summarized by some suggestions to content area teachers.

1. Learn to use a simple readability formula as an aid in evaluating text material for student use.

2. Wherever possible, provide text materials containing the essential facts, concepts, and values of the subject at varying levels of readability within the reading range of the students.

3. Don't assume that matching readability level of material to reading achievement level of students results in automatic comprehension. Remember that there are many other factors that affect reading difficulty besides those measured by readability formulas.

4. Don't assume that rewriting text materials according to readability criteria results in automatic reading ease. Leave rewriting of text material to the linguists, researchers, and editors who have time to analyze and validate their manipulations.

5. Recognize that using a readability formula is no substitute for instruction. Assigning is not teaching. Subject area textbooks are not designed for independent reading. The best way to enhance reading comprehension in your subject area is to provide the kind of instruction which prepares stu-

dents for the reading assignment, guides them in their reading, and reinforces the new ideas through rereading and discussion.

References

Burmeister, L. *Reading Strategies for Secondary School Teachers.* Reading, Mass.: Addison-Wesley, 1974.

Dale, E., and J. Chall. "A Formula for Predicting Readability." *Educational Research Bulletin,* vol. 27 (1948), pp. 11-20, 37-54.

Dawkins, J. *Syntax and Readability.* Newark, Del.: International Reading Association, 1975.

Flesch, R. *How to Test Readability.* New York, N.Y.: Harper and Row, 1951.

Fry, E. "A Readability Formula That Saves Time." *Journal of Reading,,* vol. 11, no. 7 (April 1968), pp. 513-16, 575-78.

Herber, H. *Teaching Reading in Content Areas.* Englewood Cliffs, N.J.: Prentice-Hall, 1970, 1978.

Herber, H. and J. Nelson. *Reading across the Curriculum: Staff Development Programs.* Homer, N.Y.: TRICA Consultants, 1977.

Klare, G. "Assessing Readability." *Reading Research Quarterly,* vol. 10, no. 1 (1974-1975), pp. 62-102.

Klare, G. "A Table for Rapid Determination of Dale-Chall Readability Scores." *Educational Research Bulletin,* vol. 31 (1952), pp. 43-47.

McLaughlin, G. "SMOG Grading—A New Readability Formula." *Journal of Reading,* vol. 12, no. 8 (May 1969), pp. 639-46.

Pearson, P.D. "The Effects of Grammatical Complexity on Children's Comprehension, Recall and Conception of Certain Semantic Relations." *Reading Research Quarterly,* vol. 10, no. 2 (1974-1975), pp. 155-92.

Robinson, H.A. *Teaching Reading and Study Strategies.* Boston, Mass.: Allyn & Bacon, 1975.

Shepherd, D.L. *Comprehensive High School Reading Methods.* Columbus, Ohio: Charles E. Merrill, 1973.

- *What are the advantages of "manipulative learning materials"?*
- *What steps can be taken to insure the integration of skills acquisition and content learning using these materials?*

MANIPULATIVE LEARNING MATERIALS: MERGING READING SKILLS WITH CONTENT AREA OBJECTIVES

Lesley Mandel Morrow
Rutgers University

Developing manipulative learning materials combines content area objectives and reading skills. Manipulative materials are designed for independent learning and provide a means for individualized instruction. Unlike the more typical workbook activities, manipulative materials are similar to a game. Since they are not consumable, they can be used repeatedly to provide the practice students need to master skills.

These materials are based on the needs of students. They are created to teach content objectives and the reading skills necessary to attain the objectives, sometimes teaching new skills, sometimes reinforcing old ones. Teachers, students, parents, and aides can all help in their preparation. When students prepare these materials for younger children or their peers, it becomes a learning experience for both, since children must understand the concepts before they can create learning material for others.

When a new skill is being taught, the manipulative learning material is introduced in a whole class lesson. The teacher teaches the lesson and demonstrates how the material is used, then it is placed in a center area for independent work.

The manipulative materials have directions written on them so that students can use them without the help of the teacher. They have some type of built-in reinforcement for students to know if their answers are correct. Each material is entirely contained in its own folder, which can be picked up and replaced on the designated shelf without difficulty.

Adapted from *Journal of Reading*, February 1982, *25*, 448-453.

The characteristics of these materials make it possible for the teacher to be free to work with individuals and small groups, while the class is actively involved independently. Often these teacher-made materials suit the needs of students better than store-bought materials. They also add warmth and a personalized touch to the classroom.

Manipulative learning materials can require convergent or divergent thought. Convergent activities are the more common. They ask the student for one correct answer and have built-in reinforcement. This provides the independent learning.

Divergent material encourages many answers for the same question. Differences in answers are often desirable. Reinforcement for divergent material is usually a written report, oral report or some type of project presented by the student. Although the student can work at divergent materials independently, feedback from the teacher is often required.

It is desirable to have both convergent and divergent materials available, to encourage both types of thinking.

Structuring the Materials

When creating an independent manipulative learning activity, try to:

1. Identify a content objective.
2. Determine the reading skill this content objective requires.
3. Develop an appropriate manipulative material that will teach or reinforce the objectives.
4. Make sure the material is appropriate for individuals or small groups.
5. In convergent materials, provide some built-in reinforcement so students can determine if their answers are correct.
6. For both convergent and divergent materials, provide an activity that shows the students' learning (for example, a pencil and paper activity, a project, a presentation).
7. Include clear, concise directions for the student to read and follow.
8. Include all materials the student needs, such as paper and pencil.
9. Make the material attractive (e.g., colorful and neat).
10. Laminate or cover all materials with clear adhesive-backed plastic to make them sturdy.
11. Provide a sturdy container for the material, such as a small box or a strong envelope. Place the title of the material on the container.
12. Make materials compact so that storage is easy.
13. Demonstrate how the materials are used before making them available to students.

The descriptions of the manipulative learning materials that follow are combinations of activities related to content and reading instruction. In each case, a content objective and a reading skill objective are being taught or reinforced. The materials were developed so that their basic design can be applied to teaching additional reading skills in other content areas.

When creating manipulative material think of the content to be taught and the reading skills it involves. Areas such as math, science, social studies, English, fine arts and the industrial arts all require the use of the following reading skills: defining new vocabulary, identifying details, main ideas and sequence of events, drawing conclusions, comparing and contrasting, identifying cause and effect relationships, classifying, and making decisions. These content areas also require study skills: using the dictionary, reference materials and library, using efficient study methods, taking efficient book and class notes, organizing to write reports, and understanding and using all parts of a book.

The activities described here deal with specific strategies for developing vocabulary and selected comprehension skills in math, industrial arts and fine arts. The lessons in math and industrial arts are convergent materials: There is only one right answer. The fine arts material allows for divergent thinking: There are many acceptable responses.

Convergent Material

Using picture clues to develop vocabulary in math.

A. Content area: Math/Geometry (the circle).

B. Reading skill: Using picture clues to grasp meaning.

C. Content objective: The student will be able to identify the following math vocabulary related to the circle: circle, congruent circles, points outside circle, circumscribed circle, quadrant, diameter, chord, radius, central angle, semicircle, tangent, inscribed circle, inscribed angle.

D. Materials and construction.

1. Draw lines to divide small cards into two equal sections. One card will be used for each vocabulary word.

2. Write a vocabulary word on the lefthand section of each card and draw a picture definition of the word on the right.

3. Cut each of the sections into two puzzle pieces using varied patterns at the division so that each drawing will fit with only its own vocabulary word.

4. Store materials in a sturdy envelope and label the envelope with the title of the activity (The Circle).

5. Prepare a set of directions for using the material and attach them to the outside of the storage envelope.

6. Place each answer on the back of its card.

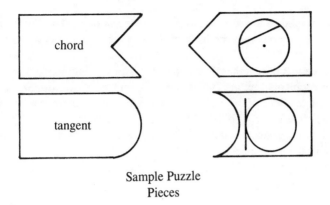

Sample Puzzle
Pieces

E. Directions for use
 1. Match the word to the symbol by fitting the puzzle pieces together.
 2. Try to think of the definition by looking at the picture first and the vocabulary word.
 3. Write down each vocabulary word and a definition you develop from the picture clue.
 4. Check your definition against the answer on the back of the card.
 5. If the definition is not clear to you, discuss it with someone.

Convergent Material
 Determining cause and effect in industrial arts.
A. Content area: Industrial arts-automotive mechanics (solve the mechanical problems).
B. Reading skill: Comprehension/inferencing – determining causes for automobile problems.
C. Content objective: When presented with the problem or effect the student will be able to diagnose the automotive mechanical causes for the problem.
D. Materials and construction.
 1. Using a manila file folder, prepare a tachistoscopic device. Open the folder and cut windows in the front and back flaps as shown in Figure 1. Label the left window "Problems" and the right window "Causes." Cut two horizontal slits in each flap – one about 1″ from the top and the other 1″ from the bottom – for the "Problem" and "Cause" strips to slide through.
 2. Cut and label a strip of paper "Problems" (Figure 2). It should be long enough to extend out the top and bottom slits in the folder. On the strip, write problems related to auto mechanics, numbering each problem; make

sure the problems can be read through the window in the flap. Put the number of each problem on the back of the strip as well, directly behind the problem.

3. Cut and label another strip of paper "Causes" (Figure 2). Write causes for the problems, putting the causes in scrambled order; do not number them. On the *back* of this strip, number each cause to correspond with the related problem.

4. Store materials in a sturdy envelope labeled with the title of the activity (Solve the Mechanical Problem).

5. Prepare a set of directions for the materials and attach them to the outside of the storage envelope.

Figure 1

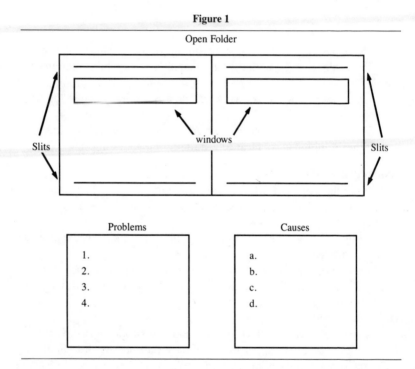

Open Folder

E. Directions for use

1. Slide the problem strip into the problem slit at the top of the folder and select a problem to diagnose by letting one appear in the window.

2. Slide the cause strip into the cause slit. Try to find the cause that diagnoses the problem by letting your choice appear in the cause window.

3. To see if you chose the correct answer, turn the folder over and check whether the numbers that appear behind the windows match. If the numbers are the same you have diagnosed the automotive problem correctly.

4. Make up your own problem-and-cause strips and leave them for others to try.

Figure 2
Sample Problems and Causes

Problems		Causes	
Loss of power	(1)*	Idle speed set too low Worn distributor rotor Incorrect ignition wiring Float level incorrect	(2)+
Engine strains	(2)*	Thin or diluted oil Low oil pressure Bent push rods Worn valve lifters	(3)+
Noisy valves	(3)*	Dirt or water in fuel line Clogged air cleaner Faulty fuel pump Faulty coil	(1)+

*this number appears on both front and back of the Problems strip

+this number appears only on the back of the Causes strip

Divergent Material

Application of information in fine arts.

A. Content area: Fine arts (create a composition).

B. Reading skill: Demonstrating literal, interpretive, and critical comprehension by applying knowledge gained from a written passage.

C. Content objective: The student will design a composition after reading a passage which describes the criteria for creating a good composition.

D. Materials and construction:

1. Prepare a passage entitled: "Creating a Good Composition."

Sample Passage
"Creating A Good Composition"
A composition is the underlying structure in art. Knowing what to include and avoid in a composition can improve a piece of work. When creating a composition try to include

some pattern of movement that does not cause a strong distraction. A composition should have a main idea and create a feeling such as happiness or sadness.

There are many things to avoid when creating a composition. Try not to center objects or corner objects. Avoid dividing objects into equal sections and try not to leave large empty spaces. Last of all, avoid symmetry.

In creating a composition it is important that it pleases you. It is impossible to do all the items that are listed above. Use the criteria only as a guide since in art there is no definite right or wrong answer.

2. Store materials in a sturdy envelope and label the envelope with the title of the activity (Creating a Good Composition).

3. Prepare a set of directions for using the materials and attach the directions to the storage envelope.

E. Directions for use.

1. Read the passage entitled "Creating a Good Composition."

2. Create a good composition by placing the felt shapes on the felt board in your own design.

3. After the composition is arranged, read the composition critique sheet and critique your design.

4. Try to improve the composition on the felt board, as suggested by the questions on the critique sheet.

5. Draw your completed design on a sheet of paper.

6. Prepare a composition critique sheet.

7. Construct a felt board (cover a piece of heavy cardboard with felt).

8. Prepare five different shapes cut from felt. Make five of each shape pictured below.

Composition Critique Sheet

(1) Is there some pattern of movement in your composition that does not cause distraction?

(2) Does your composition have a main idea? Identify it.

(3) What feeling is created as you observe your composition?

(4) Does your composition avoid the following:
   a. leading your eyes to one corner of the board?
   b. centering?
   c. cornering objects?
   d. dividing objects into sections?
   e. leaving empty spaces?
   f. using symmetry?

(5) How do you feel about your composition?

(6) Based on the answers that you have given, make changes in your composition if you feel they are necessary for improvement.

The ideas presented here are easily applied to other content areas and other skills. The geometry puzzle can be adapted to most content areas. For example, students could match science vocabulary words to their definitions or to drawings. The tachistoscope in the industrial arts activity could be used for questions and answers in social studies or matching foreign language vocabulary to English meanings. Some additional formats for developing other manipulative learning materials as skill builders are card games, Concentration, Password, crossword puzzles and word searches.

If we believe that we are teachers of students first and content second, and if students are missing basic skills needed to learn content, it is our responsibility to teach those skills. Manipulative learning materials provide an additional teaching method.

SPECIFIC SKILLS INSTRUCTION

It has been argued that the person best able to determine the specific skills students require for successful content area learning is the content area teacher. In the first instance, the content area teacher knows the content and the objectives for teaching this content—what is to be taught and the perspective from which this teaching will proceed. Through a procedure of simulating the learning process, the knowledgeable teacher is able to determine the skills students must employ to comprehend and apply the often conceptually dense and difficult reading material they face in the content area classroom. Once these skills are determined and assessed, student strengths and weaknesses are revealed. It is at this point that the teacher has the information to undertake focused instruction aimed at teaching those skills which students need to be taught.

These skills will be as diverse as the particular content area objectives which will call them into play and the various learning situations in which they will be used. It is impossible in this short book to provide direction in the teaching of every reading and study skill a content area teacher might find necessary to teach. Even if this were possible, the specific demands of particular learning situations would alter the manner and mode of instruction from any firm guidelines an author may wish to set down.

The key, then, is adaptation. Although general directions for skills instruction can be given with relative ease, the actual implementation of these directions calls for creativity and ingenuity on the part of each teacher. Teachers must adapt skills instruction to their own situations, modifying and altering the directions given here to fit the needs of their students in their own particular instructional settings. The specific demands of particular students in different schools learning in various content areas combine to place in the hands of teachers responsibility for deciding which skills are taught, and when and how they are taught.

Despite this diversity, there is one constant: In the teaching of skills (whichever ones they may be), the common denominator of effective instruction is that teaching is student centered. While the skills taught will vary widely, the manner in which they are taught will not. For students to learn the skills they need, they must be involved in the learning process and must have a clear perception of the purpose for this learning. Simply running students through a set of contrived "skills building" exercises, even if based on content area reading material, will do nothing but bore and alienate them. Rather, students must be involved in the process of learning — they must become the center of learning — by making skills instruction an integral part of the learning of content. When students see skills development as the doorway to successful content learning, they will be participative rather than passive learners. This is the kind of active, student centered participation that skills instruction must be aimed toward if it is to be successful. It is this integrative thrust among students, skills, and content that provides the foundation for successful content area skills instruction.

The articles in this section give teachers the basis for this integration. When adapted to the demands of students' particular learning situations, they provide the basis for teaching some of the skills students frequently find difficult. In the first article, Kaplan and Tuchman challenge the effectiveness of some traditional methods of vocabulary development, and in their place provide five effective strategies to further vocabulary learning. In the next article, which focuses on students' comprehension, Olson and Longnion outline various types of study guides teachers can develop to direct students' understanding of difficult content material. Next, Bromley (nee D'Angelo) illustrates ways to develop students' précis writing and points to the benefits to be derived from combining reading and writing activities. Following this, Memory and Moore outline a classroom procedure for furthering students' skimming and critical reading abilities and, in so doing, draw attention to these important, yet often overlooked, skills. Finally, Fry defends the place of graphical literacy in content area teaching and shows how this type of literacy relates to both teaching and comprehension from conventional text.

- *What four conventional methods for teaching vocabulary are rejected and why?*
- *How does each of the alternate strategies suggested contribute to vocabulary development?*

VOCABULARY STRATEGIES BELONG IN THE HANDS OF LEARNERS

Elaine M. Kaplan
Dowling College
Anita Tuchman
Westbury, New York

One of the most crucial aspects of gaining meaning from textbook reading is knowledge of content vocabulary. Students who have learned strategies for unlocking unknown words can deal more effectively in content area assignments. Yet traditionally, the teaching of vocabulary has been teacher-directed.

The options generally presented to students include: (1) The teacher selects a word list to give to the students prior to reading. This list, at best, represents the teacher's assessment of words that will be difficult for the students. Obviously, a teacher cannot predict all the words needed by all the students. Since these words are presented in isolation, out of context, they will not be readily recalled when needed. (2) The teacher directs youngsters to use a dictionary when they come across an unfamiliar word. Here one assumes students know how to extract effectively the appropriate meaning from the dictionary. Concentration and memory suffer when a youngster is forced to interrupt reading to consult a dictionary. (3) Students are told to ask the teacher the meaning of unknown words. Teachers using this "ask me" approach need to establish an environment in their classrooms where youngsters feel free to interrupt the teacher. Teachers must also question the validity of this strategy if they are attempting to develop independence in learners. Who will the child ask if the teacher is not around? (4) The teacher instructs students to use context. Learning vocabulary through use of context clues is an invaluable technique. However,

Adapted from *Journal of Reading*, October 1980, *24*, 32-40.

teachers must realize that developing expertise in this strategy requires much classroom practice using specific content area materials.

We have found that the most successful strategies for dealing with vocabulary are those that will ultimately lead students to become independent learners. The following strategies teach students to assume responsibility for their vocabulary development in content area material. For this independence to be developed, teachers should use textbook material they expect students to read as the vehicle for teaching the skills. In this way, the techniques become relevant. In order for the various strategies to become internalized by the student, much practice and repetition are necessary. Furthermore, when given considerable practice, students will sense the importance the teacher places on the learning of these techniques.

Strategy 1

Before reading a new selection, students look at chapter titles and headings. From these the students predict words that will be included in the selection. Words are noted on the board and youngsters report, after doing their assignment, whether those words were, in fact, found in the reading. Here, the emphasis is on encouraging students to use words *they* think are related rather than words the teacher has chosen. Students use their own experience and information to bring something to the topic, realizing how prior knowledge applies to new learning.

In our experience some students are either unable or unwilling to volunteer words or ideas. One of the purposes of the following strategies is to help students develop their ability to associate words freely. Another purpose is for students to use content area vocabulary in a paragraph so that they can see how words can be meaningful when related as a whole rather than used as isolated items, out of context.

Strategy 2

Teacher: "When I think about the environment, it reminds me of pollution." (Teacher writes the word "pollution" on board and turns to group.) "Pollution reminds you of...." (Teacher asks for student response.)

Student 1: "Recycling." (Write word on the board.)

Teacher: "Recycling reminds *you* of...." (Teacher points to another student.)

Student 2: "Saving paper." (Teacher writes this response on board.)

Continue in this manner until approximately ten words are listed. Provide frequent group practice in this activity using different beginning cue words. If the teacher accepts responses without judging the words, even the most reluctant students will become willing participants.

Strategy 3

Select any appropriate concept word(s) related to your area of study, i.e., women's rights, nuclear power, avarice, etc. Write the word(s) on the board and tell students they have two minutes to write down as many words as they can that relate to the subject word(s). Have several youngsters share their word lists with the group. Those students who have less than eight words on their list can make additions as classmates read their word lists. Finally, students write a paragraph using their words.

Strategy 4

Predicting the meaning of a word using context clues is extremely useful to independent learners. The teacher selects one appropriate and generally unfamiliar word from the content. Develop a title using the unknown word along with several sentences (about 7-10) that will give clues as to its meaning. Using an overhead projector, flash first the title and then one sentence at a time on the screen. Students make predictions about the meaning of the "mystery word." As the story unfolds, sentence by sentence, students find themselves verifying, modifying or rejecting their definition. This technique can be used with individuals, small groups, or the whole class.

Strategy 5

The prediction strategy is also useful when dealing with words of multiple meanings, since students are often faced with common words that have different meanings in different disciplines (e.g., table, bank, force or spring). This can lead to confusion and misinterpretation. Have students fold a piece of paper into four columns. (See Strategy 5 worksheet.) Select several words that have multiple meanings from students' textbooks and write them in the first column. Ask students to write their predictions for the meaning of each word in the next column without seeing the word in context. Students then read the paragraphs containing the defined words. If the definition remains the same, a check is placed in the third column. If, however, based on the reading, the initial definition does not make sense, students write in the appropriate definition. In the last column students list all clue words from the selection that could help to define the words.

The techniques described give students a "way in" when dealing with unknown words. In each strategy learners are asked to make some type of initial prediction or association which actively involves them in the learning process. This commitment sparks interest, giving students a reason for staying with the activity. A far cry from the passivity of word lists! After much practice, these strategies should become an integral part of the student's approach to unlocking word meaning. Each student will be able to use them on an independent basis. Vocabulary strategies will then be back where they belong—in the hands of the learner.

Strategy 5 Worksheet

Word	Predicted meaning	After reading	Clue words
ruler	something used to measure	person who controls subjects	king, crown
product	goods for sale	✓	markets, ports, goods, volume

- *What are the five steps to be taken to develop study guides?*
- *How can the kinds of guide illustrated be modified for use in different content areas?*

PATTERN GUIDES: A WORKABLE ALTERNATIVE FOR CONTENT TEACHERS

Mary W. Olson
Southwest Texas State University

Bonnie Longnion
Texas Lutheran College

For many secondary content teachers, the textbook is the one instructional aid which is extensively, and sometimes exclusively, used. The textbook provides structure for the course and contains the content to be learned.

In spite of these positive features, most content teachers are justifiably concerned with students' poor comprehension of expository material. Although textbooks must serve students with diverse reading abilities, they are often too complex for poor readers. When the concept load is considered, even able readers can have difficulty. Thus material with a single readability level and a heavy concept load produces such a mismatch between text and reader that good instruction is a formidable task.

One effective strategy to increase student understanding of the text is to provide a pattern guide, which is a specific kind of study guide. Generally teachers create guides to meet three needs: Study guides help students with poor reading skills; they focus students' attention on the reading/thinking processes required for comprehending the text, and they help students identify and locate important concepts. The pattern guide specifically addresses the relationship among the author's organization structure, the reading/thinking skills the student needs in order to comprehend the material, and the important concepts (Herber, 1978).

The relationships within the subject matter determine the author's specific pattern. When Niles (1965) analyzed a sample of secondary text-

Adapted from *Journal of Reading,* May 1982, *25,* 736-741.

books, she found that comparison/contrast, time order, cause/effect, and simple listing were the prevailing organizational schemes. Meyer and Freedle (1979) determined similar text structures—e.g., adversative (contrastive pattern), covariance (cause-effect pattern), response (problem-solution pattern), and attributive (list-like pattern). They recommend that students identify and use the author's organizational pattern to direct their efforts to understand and remember information from the text. However, within each section or chapter of a text, more than one pattern may be evident.

This article delineates the steps to create a pattern guide using Niles' labels. It also examines the organization and format of several pattern guides.

Figure 1
Structure Words

Paragraph pattern	Structure words
simple listing	for example, for instance, specifically, another, besides, also, in addition, moreover, furthermore
cause/effect	consequently, therefore, thus, as a result, however, hence
contrast/compare	on the other hand, but, by contrast, yet, in particular
time order	another, additionally, next, first, second, etc., then, and, furthermore, also

Procedure

1. Identify the essential concepts to be taught. For the most part, effective teachers present a few concepts thoroughly instead of many concepts slightly.

2. Read the appropriate section of the text, outlining, taking notes, and underlining the portions of the material which correspond to the concepts you called essential. Note the precise location of each concept in order to help students adequately.

3. Identify the organizational pattern the author used. This pattern may be implicit, lacking structure words which reflect the inherent relationships of the text. In contrast, an explicit pattern uses structure words. For example, some words signal a cause/effect writing pattern, such as *consequently, as a result,* and *therefore; besides, moreover, also,* and *another* signal a simple listing pattern. Figure 1 suggests some structure words which help us determine organizational pattern.

4. Integrate the essential concepts, the author's writing pattern, and the reading/thinking skills the student will use. For example, the class might explore the characteristic of expeditions by comparing Admiral Byrd's travels to the North Pole and the Lewis and Clark venture in Northwest America; the author may have used a contrast/compare writing pattern, and the students will need to contrast and compare aspects in reading and thinking. Or perhaps the causes of the Civil war are the essential ideas; the writing may be organized by cause/effect; and the students need to determine causal relationships.

5. The teacher determines how much help and direction to give the students in completing the pattern guide. Some students may only need to know which section of the text the information is in; other students may need specific page numbers. Poor readers will need page and paragraph number and sometimes even the line number. Your goal is to increase the student's comprehension of the textbook, so provide as much detailed assistance as the student needs.

Having moved through the five preliminary steps, you are now ready to compose the pattern guide. Brunner and Campbell (1978) offer advice: Provide for content and process; have clear and concise directions; do not overcrowd the guide; and challenge the students. With these suggestions in mind, we will examine several guides.

Formats

Figure 2 shows a format for the cause/effect writing pattern. The reading/thinking process is identified at the upper left of the guide and again in the directions, alerting the students to causal relationships in the textbook. The paragraph numbers as well as page numbers are given.

Figure 3 depicts another format suitable for a cause/effect pattern guide. The student must understand the nature of the causal links between events to complete this guide, which offers only page numbers as help.

Figures 4 and 5 portray guides for the contrast/compare and the listing pattern. The format in Figure 4 reflects the comparisons of the relationships in the history text. The hint is included to keep students on the right track. On the other hand, Figure 5 gives even more help. The first three answers are already completed. This assistance encourages the timid student and models appropriate responses.

Remember that the guide's format will vary according to the author's organizational pattern and the resulting reading/thinking process. Thus Figures 6 and 7 suggest two models for sequencing events from a textbook.

Figure 6 uses a time line, exact time frames, and page numbers to provide more assistance for the students than Figure 7. By contrast, Figure 7 does not provide dates or specific pages, although it does require sequencing of events. Figure 7 is geared for a more able reader than is Figure 6.

Figure 2
"Kinetic Theory" Chapter 12

Cause/Effect

The kinetic theory explains the effects of heat and pressure on matter. Several ramifications of the theory are discussed in this chapter. Be alert to *causal relationships* as you read.

1. Gas exerts pressure on its container because
    A. p.261, par. 1 _____
    B. p.261, par. 1 _____

2. What causes pressure to be exerted in each arm of the manometer?
    A. p. 261 -262 _____
    B. _____

3. The effects of colliding molecules which have unequal kinetic energy is _____ p. 266

4. What causes the particles of liquid to assume the shape of the container?
    p. 269, par. 1 _____

Pattern guide created from *Chemistry, a Modern Course* (Smoot & Price, 1975).

Figure 3
"Organizing the Forces of Labor" Chapter 20

Cause/Effect

In this section, look for cause-effect relationships in the situations mentioned below. Add the cause or effect in the proper column.

Cause	Effect
1.	1. Saving money was difficult or impossible for unskilled labor (p. 400).
2. Owners felt it was necessary to keep labor costs as low as possible (p. 400).	2.
3.	3. Only the boldest workers dared to defy management and join a labor organization (p. 400).
4. By 1800s wages of unskilled workers exceeded skilled artisans (p. 401).	4.
5.	5. The workingmen's parties supported Jackson after 1828 (p. 402-3).

Pattern guide created from *The Adventures of the American People* (Craft & Krout, 1970).

Figure 4
"The United States Divided" Chapter 14

Contrast/Compare

Using pages 264-265, you will contrast and compare the repercussions in the South and the North to the Supreme Court's decision in the Dred Scott case.

the South	the North
1. (Hint: newspapers)	1.
2. (Hint: Democratic Party)	2.
3.	3.
4.	4.

Pattern guide created from *The Adventures of the American People* (Craft & Krout, 1970).

Figure 5
"Sleep, Fatigue, and Rest" Chapter 4

Listing

This section of your textbook *lists* many causes of fatigue (p. 96-97). Some of the causes are physical and some are mental. Fill in the causes under the appropriate heading.

I. Physical causes of fatigue
   A. short burst of intense effort
   B. rapid growth
   C. lack of important food
   D. pg. 96, par. 3
   E.
   F.
   G.

II. Mental causes of fatigue
   A. pg. 96, par. 1
   B.

Pattern guide created from *Investigating Your Health* (Miller, Rosenberg, & Stackowski, 1971).

Figure 6
"Religious Change in Western Europe" Unit 4, Chapter 3

Time Order

A time line is an excellent way to see the sequence of events. As you read about the religious leaders (pp. 229-236), fill in the events on the time line below. Write what happened under the date.

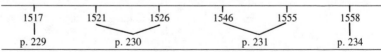

Pattern guide created from *People and Our World: A Study of World History* (Kownslar, 1977).

Olson and Longnion

Figure 7
"A Time of Conflict" Unit 4, Chapter 4

Time Order

Religious factions caused by the Reformation triggered a number of religious wars in the 1500s and 1700s. Rewrite the events below in the order they occurred. Place the date of each event beside it (pp. 237-248).

1. The son of King Charles I was called back to England for the return of the monarchy.

1.

2. The Thirty Years War involved almost all major European countries.

2.

3. Most people in the northern half of the Spanish Netherlands became Protestant.

3.

4. In England, conflict between the king and Parliament led to Civil War.

4.

5. Sweden revolted against the Catholic king of Denmark and declared its independence.

5.

6. The Act of Succession was agreed to by William and Mary.

6.

Pattern guide created from *People and Our World: A Study of World History* (Kownslar, 1977).

Teachers may expand study guides beyond the models presented here to include a variety of features. The type of study guide and the type of student determine many of the features. Possible ingredients include the purpose of the guide or an initial section devoted to vocabulary expansion and concept building. Some guides ask prereading questions; others ask postreading questions. Reinforcing activities or additional readings may supplement a well-planned guide. The length of the guide may vary from quite extensive to very brief. Independent or group activities may constitute a portion of the guide.

Realizing that generating any study guide is time consuming, Tutolo (1977) recommends that teachers reuse them each year as the need arises. He also states that the sections of the text which contain the difficult and important concepts are likely candidates for study guides. The time and effort you invest thus pay dividends repeatedly.

This article focuses on one kind of study guide, the pattern guide. The teacher perceives the author's writing pattern and the students' related reading/thinking skills in order to help them learn important content concepts. Whether teachers use study guides often or rarely, or create extensive or meager guides, study guides are an excellent instructional strategy, helping students at all levels master the essential concepts of the textbook.

References

Brunner, Joseph F. and John J. Campbell. *Participating in Reading: A Practical Approach.* Englewood Cliffs, N.J.: Prentice-Hall, 1978.

Craft, Henry and John Krout. *The Adventure of the American People.* Chicago, Ill.: Rand McNally, 1970.

Herber, Harold L. *Teaching Reading in Content Areas.* 2nd ed. Englewood Cliffs, N.J.: Prentice-Hall, 1978.

Kownslar, Allan O. *People and Our World: A Study of World History.* New York, N.Y.: Holt, Rinehart and Winston, 1977.

Meyer, Bonnie J.F. and Roy Freedle. *The Effects of Different Discourse Types on Recall.* Princeton, N.J.: Educational Testing Services, 1979.

Miller, Benjamin F., Edward B. Rosenberg, and Benjamin L. Stackowski. *Investigating Your Health.* Boston, Mass.: Houghton Mifflin, 1971.

Niles, Olive. "Organization Perceived." In *Developing Study Skills in Secondary Schools,* edited by Harold Herber. Newark, Del.: International Reading Association, 1965.

Smoot, Robert C. and Jack Price. *Chemistry, A Modern Course.* Columbus, Ohio: Charles E. Merrill Publishing, 1975.

Tutolo, Daniel J. "The Study Guide—Types, Purpose and Value." *Journal of Reading,* vol. 20 (March 1977), pp. 503-07.

- *What three things should students be taught to enable them to write précis?*
- *How does précis writing contribute to content area reading comprehension?*

PRÉCIS WRITING: PROMOTING VOCABULARY DEVELOPMENT AND COMPREHENSION

Karen D'Angelo Bromley
State University of New York at Binghamton

Recent research suggests that the development of writing skills can enhance the development of reading skills (Abartis & Collins, 1980; Lehr, 1981; Shanahan, 1980; Stotsky, 1982; Wilson, 1981). Few reading teachers, however, seem to realize the possibilities for using writing activities to help reading (Stotsky, 1982).

Nearly all written composition, especially in the content areas, deals in some way with reading. Content area writing usually grows out of responses to the informational material contained in content texts, as well as to fiction and nonfiction from library shelves. Students typically write notes, outlines, summaries, research reports, and personal essays in response to content materials.

Learning to use the skills involved in content area writing can promote the development of skills in reading comprehension. Précis writing, although used less frequently by teachers than some other activities, warrants close scrutiny because of its rich potential for promoting vocabulary development and comprehension (Stotsky, 1982).

A précis is "a paraphrase of someone else's writing that condenses the original but retains its information, emphasis, and point of view" (Ebbitt & Ebbitt, 1978, p. 599). It is a written composition that abstracts or summarizes the essence of an original sample. An acceptable length for a précis is usually considered to be less than one-third the length of the original (Leggett, Mead, & Charvat, 1978).

Précis Writing

Précis writing involves not only reading and understanding a sample of text, but also selecting, rejecting, and paraphrasing ideas in order to write a

Adapted from *Journal of Reading*, March 1983, *26*, 534-539.

concise abridgement of that sample. Processing information while reading, in order to comprehend and produce that information in writing, depends upon the ability to choose important ideas, discard unimportant ideas, and accurately restate identified concepts. Developing skills in précis writing closely relates to developing skills in reading comprehension.

The tasks involved in précis writing improve students' memory for and comprehension of content area material. Results of one study indicated that generating written summary statements while reading textbook material enhanced sixth graders' recall and comprehension (Doctorow, Wittrock, & Marks, 1978). Comprehension was improved even more for the low ability readers than for the high ability readers. In another study, sixth grade students wrote a one-sentence summary after each paragraph, while reading social studies material (Taylor & Berkowitz, 1980). Generating summaries improved memory in general and recall of main ideas, more than did merely answering teacher questions.

Gagné (1978), in a review of research on long term memory, indicates that "any strategy that encourages the elaboration of information should improve long term retention of that information" (p. 648). She states further than repetition of information strengthens and increases memory for it. Reader (1980), in a second review, reports that the generation of "semantically useful elaborations" (p. 10) and attention to "aspects of the passage that are deemed important" (p. 11) result in better retention of information. She urges teachers to have students isolate those aspects of text that seem important, and then elaborate upon them.

These data suggest that the generation processes involved in constructing "semantically useful elaborations" from text, i.e., the processes of selecting, rejecting, and paraphrasing to compose a written précis, can positively influence comprehension as well as memory.

The ability to write a précis is an important skill in which students need specific instruction. Précis writing is "an exercise of the highest value in vocabulary building, in sentence construction, and in clear, concise expression" (Hood, 1967, p. 2). It calls for "practice, hard work and considerable skill" (Ebbitt & Ebbitt, 1978, p. 59). In addition, Armbruster and Anderson (1981) warn that students must be carefully trained to use a study skill such as précis writing.

The remainder of this article discusses the specific tasks involved in précis writing, how these tasks promote reading comprehension, and ways of teaching these tasks.

Selecting and Rejecting Ideas

Identifying the main ideas of paragraphs is often difficult for both teachers and students. Donlan (1980) found that the majority of his students consistently identified the first sentence of the paragraph as the main idea, whether or not the main idea appeared there. When the main idea was not given in the first sentence, the students generally failed to locate it.

Students must be able to locate the important ideas in a passage before beginning to write a précis. They need to know that, when stated, a main idea is often expressed in a topic sentence, which can appear anywhere in a paragraph, states the central thought or important idea, and is supported by the other sentences.

Burmeister (1974) suggests that teachers use graphic shapes to illustrate possible location of topic sentences in paragraphs. Five shapes represent their locations.

∇ = topic sentence at beginning of paragraph

$\triangle$ = topic sentence at end of paragraph

$\times$ = topic sentences at beginning and end

$\Diamond$ = topic sentence within paragraph

$\bigcirc$ = topic sentence not stated

Students should practice selecting topic sentences and rejecting sentences that contain unimportant ideas in all of these paragraph types. For this practice, use paragraphs or entire selections from content area materials or nonfiction passages from basal readers. Reproduce the passages and have students first identify and underline sentences that contain main ideas, and then in the margin draw the shape that illustrates their location.

Accurate selection of the main idea sentences can be difficult. Rejecting sentences that do not contain main ideas requires students to recognize the difference between a general idea and information that may be details, examples, or simply of lesser importance. Students should look for the most general and inclusive sentence in the paragraph. The remaining sentences should provide specific information that supports this topic sentence or should provide examples to illustrate it.

In the following paragraphs, topic sentences are in italics and appropriate shapes illustrate their location. Paragraphs such as these could be used to give a group of students oral practice in choosing topic sentences. A discussion of the reasons for selecting a certain topic sentence should help develop this skill.

∇ *Scientists, called entomologists, study insects to find out what they eat, where they grow, and where they lay their eggs.* They try to find out which insects are harmful to plants and animals and which are helpful. Most entomologists work in laboratories. There they have tools and equipment to help them study insects very closely. Their work helps beekeepers raise bees that will make more and better tasting honey. (*Time to Wonder,* Holt, 1980.)

△ A mayfly, though it lives as a fly but a day or so, has a life of light and air and dancing. A clam can live for twenty years, but who wants to be a clam? A salamander may live for fifty years, but it doesn't see much of the world. An eagle can live that long, too. But soaring over mountain and forest, it reaches heights of adventures and experience impossible to the cold-blooded salamanders. So, length is no measure for life. *It is what you get out of life and what you put into it that matters. (Time to Wonder,* Holt, 1980.)

⋎ *Another animal under the rock looks like a thick, gray lump.* It is a slug. When it crawls, it stretches out and becomes long and thin. There are long feelers on its head that look like horns. Its body is slick and slippery when you touch it. The feelers and the way it moves make you think of a snail. *A slug is a kind of snail without a shell. (Hand Stands,* Allyn and Bacon, 1978, first published by McGraw-Hill Book Company, 1971.)

⋏ On the second pair of legs, at each joint, there are also rows of very fine hairs. *These hairs are the daddy longlegs' "ears."* This hearing can be tested by making a loud noise near a daddy longlegs. Its second pair of legs will jerk right away. (*Time to Wonder,* Holt, 1980.)

◯ But that is old, very old, for an animal. The record age for a horse is fifty years. For an owl, it's sixty-eight. The record age for a dog is twenty-two, for a toad twenty, for a lobster fifty, for a pelican fifty-one. And for a bullfrog it is sixteen. (*Time to Wonder,* Holt, 1980.)

Paraphrasing and Writing Ideas

Following selection of appropriate topic sentences, main ideas need to be restated or paraphrased in a shortened version. Merely copying passages verbatim from text does not result in better comprehension than paraphrasing and writing summaries. Better comprehension results when students make a greater cognitive effort and process information more deeply by using their own words to elaborate on the text and paraphrase its important ideas (Bretzing & Kulhavy, 1979).

Students should supply synonyms for key words in topic sentences. Both a dictionary and a thesaurus are valuable for this task. Training in paraphrasing can result in vocabulary growth measurable both in quantity of words and in quality or variety of words recognized and used by students in listening, speaking, reading, and writing.

Before students are asked to rephrase topic sentences in writing, oral practice is important. When students have opportunities as a group to supply words similar to those in text, and discuss their choices, skill with rephrasing develops more easily. The actual writing of paraphrased ideas then becomes an extension of what students do orally.

In the "Peanuts" selection (Schultz, 1973) topic sentences are in italics and appropriate shapes are included. Following it is a précis written by a fourth grade group in which the synonyms they supplied for vocabulary used by the author are also in italics.

"Peanuts—How It All Began"
by Charles M. Schultz

◇ When I was growing up, the three main forms of entertainment were Saturday afternoon
▽ movies, the late afternoon radio programs, and the comic strips. *I grew up with only one
real desire in life—and that was someday to draw my own comic strip.* With me, it was not
a matter of how I became a cartoonist, but merely a matter of when. I am quite sure that if
I had not sold "Peanuts" when I did, I would have sold something eventually, and that even
to this day, if I had not yet sold something, I would continue to draw because I had to.

▽ *During the last year I was in high school, I began to take a course by mail from Art
△ Instruction School, which is located in Minneapolis.* I finished their course in two years
and then began to send in cartoons. It was not until I returned from World War II that I
made my first sale of some kid cartoons to our local newspaper in St. Paul. I also was
finally able to break through in the Saturday Evening Post with about fifteen gag cartoons.
And then one day in 1949 I sold "Peanuts" to United Feature Syndicate.

◇ This is how it all happened, and if I look back upon it now, *it all seems quite simple.* But I
▽ imagine this is because memory has a way of knocking off the corners.

▽ *There is no doubt in my mind that drawing a comic strip has to be the best job in the
△ world.* People send you wonderful letters, the company for which you work sends you
enough money to live on, and you are allowed to draw all of the pictures that you have
been wanting to draw ever since you were a little kid. You also are given an outlet for all of
your emotions. Every feeling that you have, plus all your experience and knowledge, go
into the creation of a comic strip. You will be surprised how your ideas get better as you
grow older. The ability to draw is not the only ability which improves with time. *The
ability to create ideas improves as you yourself grow up.*

Sample précis

Charles M. Schultz grew up with only one *true wish* and that was to draw a comic strip.
When he was a *senior* in high school he took a drawing course by mail and a few years
later sold some cartoons and the famous "Peanuts" cartoon. He feels that *success* came
easily for him. Schultz says that drawing cartoons is a job *unequalled* by any other job
because of the *rewards*. Schultz feels that skill in *inventing* new *concepts* improves as you
age.

The précis is the result of several lessons in each of the following: selecting topic sentences, identifying paragraph shapes, using synonyms, and
rephrasing. The actual writing of the précis itself involves the least amount
of time. As Armbruster and Anderson (1981) conclude, students need to
be carefully trained in order to learn to use any study technique effectively.
Teachers and students alike should be aware that writing a précis is indeed
difficult, requiring practice and the learning of several skills.

Students must remember three key things to help them write an accurate
and concise précis: Identify topic sentences, rephrase in your own words,
and as you write, keep the order of the text.

As students become proficient in précis writing, it is not necessary to keep the order of the text intact. Often changing the sequence of ideas or information will clarify a passage. Also, emphasis can be shifted from one point to another by focusing attention on an idea mentioned first or saved for last. When first learning to write a précis, however, students find the process simpler if the original order of the text is retained.

Benefits of Précis Writing

Skill in précis writing can benefit students in several ways. Students who learn to write an accurate and concise précis possess a skill which is useful for reports and research papers, two activities they will be involved in throughout their school years. In addition, précis writing helps students study for tests. As each chapter in a content text is read, a précis of it can be written and these summaries kept for review in preparation for tests.

In addition to improving research skills and providing material to study for tests, the daily writing of summaries increases students' attention in class and improves spelling of content area vocabulary according to Cunningham and Cunningham (1976). These researchers reported that their students became better writers in general when they had daily practice in writing summaries. The quantity and quality of receptive vocabularies (listening and reading) and expressive vocabularies (speaking and writing) improve as students become skilled in précis writing.

When students engage in "semantically useful elaborations" of text, comprehension, long term memory, and learning in general are positively affected. Writing a précis is one way of elaborating meaningfully on text. The technique warrants use with students, since it integrates reading with writing and possesses such rich potential for developing both vocabulary and comprehension.

References

Abartis, Caesarea, and Cathy Collins. "The Effect of Writing Instruction and Reading Methodology upon College Students' Reading Skills." *Journal of Reading,* vol. 23 (February 1980), pp. 408-13.

Armbruster, Bonnie, and Thomas Anderson. "Research Synthesis on Study Skills." *Educational Leadership,* vol. 39 (November 1981), pp. 154-56.

Bretzing, Burke H., and Raymond W. Kulhavy. "Notetaking and Depth of Processing." *Contemporary Educational Psychology,* vol. 4 (April 1979), pp. 145-54.

Burmeister, Lou E. *Reading Strategies for Secondary School Teachers.* Reading, Mass.: Addison-Wesley, 1974, pp. 161-63.

Cunningham, Patricia, and James Cunningham. "SSSW, Better Content Writing." *Clearinghouse,* vol. 49 (January 1976), pp. 237-38.

Doctorow, Marleen, M.C. Wittrock, and Carolyn Marks. "Generative Processes in Reading Comprehension." *Journal of Educational Psychology,* vol. 70 (1978), pp. 109-18.

Donlan, Dan. "Locating Main Ideas in History Textbooks." *Journal of Reading*, vol. 24 (November 1980), pp. 135-41.

Ebbitt, Wilma R., and David R. Ebbitt. *Writer's Guide and Index to English*. Glenview: Ill.: Scott, Foresman, 1978.

Gagné, Ellen D. "Long-term Retention of Information Following Learning from Prose." *Review of Educational Research*, vol. 48 (Fall 1978), pp. 629-65.

Hand Stands. Level 14. Boston, Mass.: Allyn and Bacon, 1978. (First published in *What We'll Find When We Look Under Rocks*, Frances Behnke, McGraw-Hill Book Company, 1971.)

Hood, Richard. *Précis Writing Practice*. Cambridge, Mass.: Educators Publishing Service, 1967.

Leggett, Glen, David Mead, and William Charvat. *Handbook for Writers*. Englewood Cliffs, N.J.: Prentice-Hall, 1978.

Lehr, Fran. "Integrating Reading and Writing Instruction." *The Reading Teacher*, vol. 34 (May 1981), pp. 958-61.

Reder, Lynne M. "The Role of Elaboration in the Comprehension and Review of Prose: A Critical Review." *Review of Educational Research*, vol. 50 (Spring 1980), pp. 5-53.

Schultz, Charles M. "Peanuts—How It All Began." *Liberty Magazine*, vol. 11 (Winter 1973), pp. 14-16, 39.

Shanahan, Timothy. "The Impact of Writing Instruction on Learning to Read." *Reading World*, vol. 19 (May 1980) pp. 357-68.

Stotsky, Sandra. "The Role of Writing in Developmental Reading." *Journal of Reading*, vol. 24 (January 1982), pp. 330-39.

Time to Wonder, Level 13. Holt Basic Reading Program. New York, N.Y.: Holt, Rinehart and Winston, 1980.

Taylor, Barbara, and Sandra Berkowitz. "Facilitating Children's Comprehension of Content Material." In *29th Yearbook of the National Reading Conference*, pp. 54-68. Washington, D.C.: National Reading Conference, 1980.

Wilson, Marilyn. "A Review of Recent Research on the Integration of Reading and Writing." *The Reading Teacher*, vol. 34 (May 1981), pp. 896-901.

● *Why is purpose setting important for skimming?*
● *How are skimming and critical reading related?*

SELECTING SOURCES IN LIBRARY RESEARCH: AN ACTIVITY IN SKIMMING AND CRITICAL READING

David M. Memory
Indiana State University

David W. Moore
University of Northern Iowa

According to a recent study, many middle and secondary school teachers feel that skimming and scanning activities and those involving distinguishing fact from opinion are among the least important of the reading activities that might be taught (Criscuolo, Vacca, & LaVorgna, 1980). Despite the infrequent use of skimming and the difficulty of teaching critical reading in a textbook-centered classroom, these skills are valuable and deserve attention. Anyone who has written a library research paper is especially well aware of their value. When you are searching for material on a particular topic, it makes no sense to plod through every potential source, diligently taking notes on everything read. Some potential sources turn out to be irrelevant or inconsequential. It is better to discover this after a skilled skim through the material than after an hour or so of wasted effort and several pages of unneeded notes. For skimming to be truly skillful, it must be combined with some of the important components of critical reading — skills such as evaluating the qualifications of an author and detecting bias in writing.

Students can learn the importance of these skills through a relatively simple and stimulating classroom activity that we have used successfully with both high school students and preservice and inservice teachers.

Adapted from *Journal of Reading*, March 1981, *24*, 469-474.

Set 1 (low average readers)

"Bring Back the Draft?" *U.S. News and World Report,* February 14, 1979, pp. 57-58. (a report suggesting a need for the draft)

"In His Own Words." *People,* July 2, 1979, pp. 31-32, 35. (an interview with Morris Janowitz, author of *The Professional Solider* and a sociology professor, favoring draft of everyone for military or civilian service)

"Let's Play Taps for an All Male Army!" by Yvonne B. Burke, *Saturday Evening Post,* October 1977, pp. 12-13, 84. (argument for a both-sex draft by a former member of Congress)

"The Military Draft: Should We Bring It Back?" and "Mandatory National Service?" *Senior Scholastic,* April 19, 1979, pp. 10-12.

"Rating the Volunteer Army." *Time,* (October 10, 1977, pp. 34,36. (a report of a Rand Corporation study giving good marks to the volunteer army)

"Young People Needed," by Harris Wofford. *Seventeen,* November 1979, pp. 160-61, 179. (an argument for national service by a cochairperson of the Committee for the Study of National Service)

Set 2 (high average and above average readers)

"Draft No, Assassins Yes," by John Garvey. *Commonweal,* August 3, 1979, pp. 425-26. (a satiric argument against the draft included as an example of a type of article not worth reading carefully as a source)

"The Draft: Why the Country Needs It," by James Fallows. *Atlantic,* April 19, 1980, pp. 44-47. (an article by the Washington editor of *Atlantic*)

"Reviving the Draft," by Robert A. Seeley, *Progressive,* June 1979, pp. 32-36. (an argument against the draft by the editor of a newsletter of a draft counseling agency)

"Staying Out of the Trenches," by Ellen Cantarow. *New Republic,* March 1, 1980, pp. 19-21. (a piece of reportage opposed to the draft by the author of *Moving the Mountain,* a study of women organizers)

"The Volunteer Army in Review," by Drew Middleton. *Atlantic,* December 1977, pp. 6, 8, 10, 12-13. (balanced, fact-filled discussion by an unidentified writer)

"Volunteer Army Runs into Trouble." *U.S. News and World Report,* March 5, 1979, p. 54 (a report of low recruiting success)

Collecting Materials

The teacher, possibly with help from students, selects a controversial topic of interest to the class. This topic should be one about which the students have only limited or superficial knowledge. Then the teacher uses *Readers' Guide* or a similar index to identify an assortment of articles on the topic. Try to locate articles from a variety of magazines—some not necessarily respected for their accuracy, some noted for the consistent bias in their writing, and some praised for their impartiality and trustworthiness. In addition, a wide range in readabiity levels is helpful, though not always possible.

From this group of sources, the teacher selects several sets of about six articles. The selections within each set should be similar in difficulty, but they should represent as much variety in viewpoint and style as possible. For the activity itself, each student must have access to one article at all times; therefore, some sets may need to be reproduced to accommodate large numbers of students at certain reading ability levels.

An example of a topic good for secondary students is that of the draft for military or other national service. Young men have always been concerned about it and women at that age are now increasingly concerned. In addition, many arguments for and against the draft are sufficiently technical to be unfamiliar to most high school students. In short, the draft typifies the type of topic that is most useful in teaching skimming, for it is a topic (1) in which most high school students are interested and (2) about which most are not well informed.

A topic's usefulness will be somewhat limited if it has not been discussed in many magazines suitable for less able readers. This is true of our example, the military draft. Therefore, the selections listed in the Figure are grouped primarily to display an appropriate variety in viewpoints as an example for teachers who are familiar with these magazines. Some readers may want to use the list in a pilot project on skimming.

The four sets of sample articles in the Figure would work well with a class of no more than 18 good readers and 6 low average readers. If a class has more low average readers, Set 1 would have to be reproduced to insure that each student has an article at all times.

Introducing the Activity

On the day before the articles are actually skimmed, the teacher introduces the objectives of the activity. In our example, the students could be told to imagine that they have been assigned a term paper on the advisability of reinstating some form of compulsory national service in the U.S. In that paper they will say whether or not the draft is again needed and why. If they favor it, they will explain who should be subject to the draft and what type of service will be involved.

In the course of this introductory discussion, the students should be reminded that people can most easily write convincingly on a topic if they are aware of and understand all of the key issues involved. Having this make-believe writing objective in mind, the students are told that their task in the simulation will be to skim a group of articles to decide which ones they would return to for a careful reading and in what order they would read the chosen articles. They will imagine that they have previously used a reference source that lists magazine articles, such as *The Reader's Guide to Periodical Literature,* to locate articles that might be useful in writing the paper. The next day's activity will give them a chance to practice their skimming and critical reading skills on some of the articles they have found.

Set 3 (high average and above average readers)

"The Draft: Why the Army Needs It," by James Webb. *Atlantic,* April 1980, pp. 34-38, 42-44. (an article by an ex-Marine infantry officer who served in South Vietnam)

"The Military as an Employer: Past Performance and Future Prospects," by Sar A. Levitan and Karen C. Alderman. *Monthly Labor Review,* December 1977, pp. 19-23. (a summary by the authors of *Warriors at Work: The Volunteer Armed Forces,* which reports research supported by the Ford Foundation on prospects for the military in competing with civilian employers for workers)

"Minimal Coercion: The Plan to Revive the Draft," by David Cortwright. *Progressive,* June 1977, pp. 25-28. (argument against the draft by the author of *Soldiers in Revolt: The American Military Today*)

"Notes on a Broken Promise," by Lucian K. Truscott IV. *Harper's,* July 1974, pp. 20-22, 26-29. (narrative discussion of the weaknesses of the volunteer Army by a guilt-ridden third-generation West Point graduate who left it; included as an example of a type of article not worth reading carefully as a source)

"Too Few Good Men," by Seth Cropsey. *Harper's,* December 1979, pp. 16, 18, 20. (an argument for the draft by a writer for *Fortune*)

"U.S. Almost Alone in Spurning Draft." *U.S. News and World Report,* March 10, 1980, p. 34.

Set 4 (high average and above average readers)

"The Drive to Revive the Draft," by Bertram M. Gross. *Nation,* October 20, 1979, pp. 353, 360-65. (argument against the draft and suggestions for action by a professor of public policy and the author of a book on "the draft in the context of the rebuilding of American militarism.")

"It Just Isn't Working," by Harry A. Marmion. *Commonweal,* October 12, 1979, pp. 555-57. (argument for the draft by an educational consultant for the American Council on Education)

"National Service and the All-Volunteer Force," by Charles C. Mockos. *Society,* November-December 1979, pp. 70-72. (argument for national service by a sociology professor and author of *Peace Soldiers*)

"Opening Pandora's Box," by Murray Polner. *Commonweal,* October 12, 1979, pp. 553-55. (argument against the draft by the author of *No Victory Parades: The Return of the Vietnam Veteran* and *When I Come Home?* about draft resisters, deserters, and exiles)

"The Volunteer Army," by Donald Smith. *Atlantic,* July 1974, pp. 6-12. (narrative description of Ft. Benning by an unidentified writer; included as an example of a type of article not worth reading carefully as a source)

"Women in the Armed Forces," by Melinda Beck. *Newsweek,* February 18, 1980, pp. 34-36, 39, 41-42. (a lengthy piece of fact-filled reportage)

Following this overview of the activity, the teacher introduces the students to or reminds them of the important steps in effective skimming. Thomas and Robinson's (1977) sourcebook on reading in content area classes provides a comprehensive discussion upon which this introduction to skimming could be based.

If this is indeed an introduction and not just a review, it is appropriate to provide each student with a copy of a sample article or to use transparencies to show the article page by page with an overhead projector. Then the teacher demonstrates how to analyze the title quickly, possibly jump ahead and read the concluding paragraph, read the introduction, and survey the introductory and closing sentences in the paragraphs of the body of the article. Since most stories in weekly news magazines are already condensed, the students are alerted that those brief articles can be read profitably from start to finish.

In addition to these suggestions, the teacher emphasizes that the nature and reputation of the author of an article are important bases for deciding whether to return to that source and read it closely. Identifying all specific points in a selection is not essential for determining its potential value as a source, but discerning the overall viewpoint of the author and the general approach used in presenting that viewpoint is important. Therefore, students are advised to take notes only on the gist of each article and on details that might be needed in comparing the selections as possible sources.

Skimming and Discussing the Articles

When the day of the activity arrives, the students are grouped with their desks arranged so that articles can be passed easily from one student to another. The grouping can be partly by reading ability if certain of the students can be expected to understand only the easier articles. To insure that every student has something to read at all times, the set of selections for each group must contain as many different articles as there are students in the group. If articles have to be copied so as to have enough for all students, the longer ones should be selected so that they can be examined adequately by at least some of the students in the group.

An alphabetized master list showing the author, title, and assigned number of each article is provided for each student. Numbers are given to the articles so that the students do not have to write out lengthy names and titles when taking notes.

Just before the skimming begins, the teacher should remind the students of the specific objectives of the activity so that the notes they take will enable them to make wise decisions about which articles to read carefully and in what order.

Six different articles per set with 4 or 5 minutes allotted to each article is a convenient arrangement for the skimming itself. For a 45-minute class period, this allows 5 minutes or so to get organized at the beginning of the period and about 15 minutes to start the follow-up discussion when the skimming is finished. At the end of each 5-minute time block, the teacher tells the students to pass their articles on to the next student. Those disappointed at having to give up an article can be reminded that this is necessary to keep the activity going and can be assured that the articles will be available for closer study later.

The discussion of the articles should begin immediately after the skimming is completed, but most of it will have to take place the next day. The first phase is centered in the individual groups. For possibly 10 minutes the students in each group share their initial reactions to the selections in their set. This sharing usually helps give students confidence about expressing their views to the whole class. In addition, during this part of the discussion, students usually agree that certain articles do not deserve mention and others should be discussed by more than one group member. The teacher should circulate among the groups to comment on these decisions.

An effective way to organize the whole-group discussion is to have each student in turn tell the class the article that he or she would most definitely want to read carefully and use as a source for the make-believe term paper. And, of course, reasons must be provided for selecting the particular article. A brief period of class discussion should follow each of these student statements. It is through this discussion that the teacher can introduce or reinforce important critical reading skills.

Since a half dozen or more students will have skimmed each article, many of the relevant points about the potential value of the selections will be made without any prompting by the teacher. Nevertheless, some important information, such as the reputation of certain magazines and certain authors, will not be known by the students. In addition, background information provided about authors is often overlooked by students accustomed to accepting textbooks and other reading materials as objective truth. Therefore, the teacher needs to be prepared to call attention to unfamiliar or overlooked facts that illustrate the types of information that competent readers use in evaluating what they read.

Follow-up Activities

Many teachers will choose to use this activity as part of an introduction to a library research project. If that is the case, then several students may want to write their papers on the topic used in the simulation. This is likely since the activity has the effect of arousing interest in an area but not fully satisfying that interest. Most teachers will welcome this result, and they need not feel that a convenient list of possible sources is too much of an aid for students who otherwise might not muster enough interest to look at more than two or three articles on a topic.

Even if a term paper is not required, this activity could be used as a way to introduce variety into classroom routines. The topic selected can be one that is normally studied in a course. Each student could select an article to read carefully and report on to the whole class, basing the decision on impressions gained during the skimming. When more than one student picks the same article, the teacher can resolve the situation by assigning difficult selections to good readers and easy selections to poor readers. If oral reports are given, the opportunities for discussion of critical reading skills become even greater than after skimming alone.

Whether or not follow-up reading and writing are used, this activity has a place in the content area classroom. With a combination of an interesting topic, articles with varied perspectives and of varying quality, and two and a half days of class time, almost any teacher of a content subject can carry out this simulation successfully. Since library research is a defensible component of almost any course, it is an activity that deserves consideration as a way to help students in skimming and critical reading.

References

Criscuolo, Nicholas P., Richard T. Vacca and Joseph J. LaVorgna. "What Reading Strategies Make Sense to Content Area Teachers?" *Reading World,* vol. 19 (March 1980), pp. 265-71.

Thomas, Ellen L., and H. Alan Robinson. *Improving Reading in Every Class: A Sourcebook for Teachers,* 2nd ed. Boston, Mass.: Allyn and Bacon, 1977.

- *What is meant by "graphic literacy"?*
- *What learning results from reading and drawing graphs?*

GRAPHICAL LITERACY

Edward Fry
Rutgers University

Graphical literacy is the ability to read and write (or draw) graphs. Isolated elements of graphical literacy already exist in most school curriculums, but as a concept it is not well developed or well taught. Some aspects of map or graph reading are taught in social studies curriculums. In a few reading courses, these simple graphical reading skills are subsumed as part of "study skills." Bits and pieces of graph drawing appear in vocational or mechanical drawing classes, mathematics classes, or in the art department. However, what I am proposing here is literacy in graphs that begins to approach word literacy.

Cognitive Psychology Background

The use of graphs to communicate information has been around since or before written verbal language. Pictures, maps, and other types of graphs have been used throughout the ages. However, educators have recently become more interested in nonverbal communication as part of the cognitive movement in psychology. Researchers have pointed out some interesting things; for example:

> In nearly all right-handers, and in about 70 percent of the left-handers, the left hemisphere (of the brain) employs an analytic, sequential strategy appropriate for verbal proposition information. The right hemisphere characteristically uses a global or holistic, synthetic or appositional strategy, such as one might use in looking at a painting, where parts acquire meaning through their relation to the whole (Whittrock, 1978).

Another cognitive psychology approach has been through the study of imagery. Paivio (1974) has found that pictures and instructions to generate images facilitate memory. Levin (1976) has found that both children and adults remember pictures of objects better than names of objects. Graphs

Adapted from *Journal of Reading*, February 1981, *24*, 383-390.

are an interesting way of presenting schemata, or as Confucius is reputed to have said, "A picture is worth a thousand words."

Figure 1
Illustration of the Taxonomy of Graphs

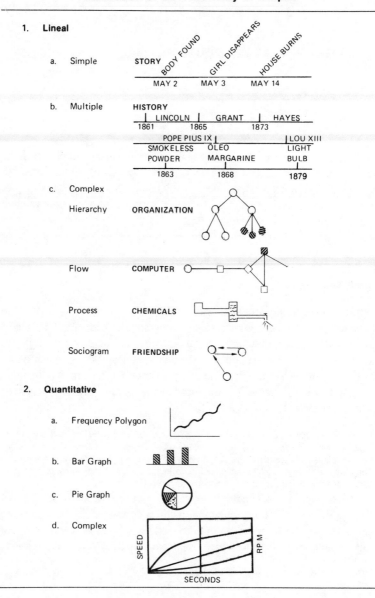

1. **Lineal**

    a. Simple

    b. Multiple

    c. Complex

       Hierarchy

       Flow

       Process

       Sociogram

2. **Quantitative**

    a. Frequency Polygon

    b. Bar Graph

    c. Pie Graph

    d. Complex

Figure 1 (continued)

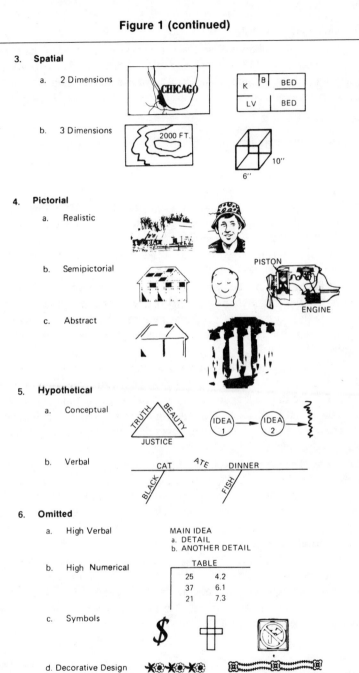

3. **Spatial**

   a. 2 Dimensions

   b. 3 Dimensions

4. **Pictorial**

   a. Realistic

   b. Semipictorial

   c. Abstract

5. **Hypothetical**

   a. Conceptual

   b. Verbal

6. **Omitted**

   a. High Verbal

   b. High Numerical

   c. Symbols

   d. Decorative Design

Reading Teacher's Role

I am proposing that reading teachers are well equipped to take active educational leadership in graphical literacy because they already have many skills that are readily transferable. For example, it is quite possible to teach map comprehension by asking such typical comprehension questions as:

> What is the main idea of this map? (To show the location of a housing tract)
>
> What details support this main idea? (Tract location in the center of the map, only roads leading to the tract clearly marked)
>
> What is the author's purpose in drawing this map? (To sell houses)
>
> How are the details interrelated? (Does road location have anything to do with rivers or mountains?)
>
> What new vocabulary is used? What new symbols? (Arroyo, off ramp) (300m, R-1 zone)

I need not go on, but perhaps already you can see that many, if not most, typical "reading comprehension" types of questions can be asked of a map. A map is only one kind of graph; many types of reading comprehension questions can also be asked of a bar graph, a time line, or other kinds of graphs.

Singer and Donlan (1980) suggest that graphs could be taught using the Directed Reading Activity (DRA), which is similar to some types of reading lessons where the teacher conducts a prereading discussion including new vocabulary and background. The student reads the graph, then does activities related to the graph including answering comprehension questions or possibly drawing similar graphics.

Reading teachers, or teachers interested in reading, are further qualified to take a leadership role in graphical literacy because they are already part of the literacy education area and part of the communication field. Their knowledge of everything from individual differences to tests and measurements can be applied, and they are used to working with material from many subject matter areas.

But before going further into graphical literacy, let us give a more complete definition of graphs with a taxonomy and some examples. Most of what I am calling graphs fall into the five areas outlined in A Taxonomy of Graphs shown in Figure 1: Lineal, Quantitative, Spatial, Pictorial, or Hypothetical. See Figure 1, Figure 2, and A Taxonomy of Graphs for details.

Figure 2
A Taxonomy of Graphs

1. *Lineal graphs* - Sequential data
   a. *Simple lineal* - For example, a time line or simple nonbranching flow chart can be used in history, literature (a story line), or directions.
   b. *Multiple lineal* - Parallel lines. For example, a set of three time lines that show terms of office of presidents, with a parallel line showing inventions, and a third parallel line that shows the reigns of English kings or queens.
   c. *Complex lineal* - Complex lines that have branching, feedback loops, and diverse data. For example, a computer programmer's flow chart; a process chart; or a hierarchy chart for a business or government organization; a geneaology chart, or a sports tournament elimination chart.

2. *Quantitative graphs* - Numerical data
   a. *Frequency polygon* - Gives continuous data, can best show trends. For example, a normal distribution curve, growth curves, stock market fluctuations.
   b. *Bar graph* - Gives discrete data points, can best show the difference between two amounts. For example, it can contrast the size of enrollment for three different years.
   c. *Pie graph* - Best shows percent by various areas.
   d. *Complex numerical graphs* - Engineering graphs, multiple data graphs, higher mathematics graphs. For example, graphs drawn in logarithmic units, multiple line, or multiple variables.

3. *Spatial graphs* - Area and location
   a. *Two-dimensional* - Represent something flat. For example, road maps, floor plans, football plays.
   b. *Three-dimensional* - Represent height or depth plus length and width. For example, a map with contour lines showing mountains or valleys, mechanical drawings, or building elevations that accurately show dimensions.
Basically, spatial graphs show the location of a point or the location and size of a line (one dimension), area (two dimensions), or volume (three dimensions). By use of special indicators or multiple graphs, different time periods can be shown.

4. *Pictorial graphs* - Visual concepts
   a. *Realistic* - More or less what the eye would see without significant distortion or elimination of detail. Can have an angle or point of view, selection of subject matter, selection of composition, background, and content. For example, photographs or realistic drawings, single or multiple color.
   b. *Semipictorial* - A recognizable image but with noticeable distortions in form, color, content, or omissions of detail. For example, most Picasso paintings, schematic drawings showing cutaway or exploded engine, cartoons, or outline drawings.
   c. *Abstract pictorial* - Highly abstracted drawing which, however remote, has some basis in visual reality. For example, a single line across a space might represent the horizon; a vertical line, a person; a series of squares, a row of automobiles. Abstract drawings or graphs nearly always require some context, verbal explanation, or prior experience with the type of abstraction.

5. *Hypothetical graphs* - Interrelationship of ideas
   These graphs have little or no basis in visual reality
   a. *Conceptual graph* - An attempt to communicate abstract ideas by using lines, circles, and other forms, with or without words or symbols. For example, a philosopher who labels the sides of a triangle "truth, beauty, justice"; a theoretical model of the reading process with boxes labeled "short-term memory and long-term memory."
   b. *Verbal graph* - The use of graphical arrangements of words or symbols to add meaning to the words. For example, a sentence diagram, semantic mapping.

6. *Intentional omissions from the Taxonomy of Graphs*
   a. *High verbal omission* - On the borderline between having some graph qualities and being purely verbal would be a typical outline with main idea and supporting details, or posters and advertisements composed with different sizes and styles of type that show emphasis or are aesthetically pleasing.
   b. *High numerical omission* - Arrangements composed mostly of numbers, such as statistical tables, are omitted.
   c. *Symbols* are omitted because, for all practical purposes, they are the equivalent of a word. Typical examples are rebuses or glyphs (like the outline of a man on a restroom door, a cross on a church building, and road sign arrows).
   d. *Decorative design* - Designs whose main purpose is decoration, not conveying concepts, are omitted.

   Combinations - Nearly any kind of graph can be combined. An example of a combination would be a mechanical drawing, which is a type of spatial graph (3b), but which could approach the reality of a picture (Section 4, Pictorial). Another example would be a bar graph, which is quantitative (2b), but which can use drawings or photographs of images; for example, car production is seen as many little cars piled on top of each other.

Graph Uses

Graphs are used because they quickly communicate a concept better than words. Even though many of them contain some words or numbers, the basic transmittal of information is nonverbal.

Graphs pack a high density of information into a small area. A very large statistical table can often be compressed into two or three simple lines on a frequency polygon graph. And even more than that, a curved line is an infinite number of points (if you remember your geometry), and theoretically every point can be read or interpreted, whereas a table necessarily has a fixed number of points. For many people, looking at a curved line shows a trend better than looking at a page of numbers.

The ability to read graphs is becoming increasingly important because they are being more widely used in newspapers, magazines, textbooks, and television presentations. Computers are learning to draw graphs in order to simplify massive amounts of statistics or complex mathematical data. Offset printing, now so widely used, makes the reproduction of graphics easier than former printing processes. Students in today's schools can look forward to an increasing use of graphical presentations on computer terminals, in print, and in classrooms.

Drawing Graphs

Reading and comprehending graphs is only half of graphical literacy. The other half is the ability to draw them. Students need to draw them so that they can better communicate ideas, so they can use them in studying, and so they can better understand them.

Drawing a graph can be a creative communicating experience similar to writing a paragraph or a story. There are many ways to express the same ideas graphically, just as a writer can express a written idea in a variety of ways. Someday we may see a course in creative graphing just as we now have creative writing. In the meantime, a unit of a reading, communications, or writing class might well be devoted to graphing.

Graphing, or expressing ideas graphically, is already a well established part of some study skills courses. It should be developed. Outlining, summarizing, notetaking, and underlining are all fine study techniques; but they are all essentially verbal. Graphing can add another very important dimension to study techniques. Once the students start to think about applying graphing whenever possible, they will be amazed at how often it can be applied.

Teachers can help to develop graphing ability by making assignments just as they now do for writing. For example, take a section of a history book, science article, or short story and ask the students to make as many graphs as they can to illustrate ideas in the material.

Another interesting lesson for teaching graphing is to take a newspaper article, budget statement, or some other piece of writing with numerical data and ask the student to attempt to make a graph. You will often find that the article does not contain enough information to draw a complete graph. The students will learn that a graph contains far more information than most typical prose paragraphs about data. Or stated another way, the graph more succinctly conveys the information.

Valuing Graphs

We teach reading and writing because we value reading and writing. We teach mathematics because we value mathematics. We will only teach graphical literacy because we value it. If we do value graphical literacy, here are some things we can do.

- Allow some time for graphical literacy in the curriculum.
- Ask reading comprehension type of questions about graphs.
- Select texts that have a good use of graphs.
- Talk to students about the importance of graphs.
- Grade graphs in student papers.
- Work on extending the types of graphs a student uses.
- Have a graphing contest and prizes.
- Invite art and drafting teachers to reading and English classes to talk about graph use and development.
- Use graphs yourself on the chalkboard or the overhead projector in explaining ideas.

Conclusion

Graphical literacy – the ability to both comprehend and draw graphs – is an important communication tool that needs more emphasis in the school curriculum. Reading teachers, by virtue of their experience teaching reading comprehension, their practice in using materials from many fields, and their knowledge of educational principles, are qualified to teach graphical literacy and aid other teachers in developing units in this subject.

Furthermore, reading teachers often teach some graphing techniques in study skills segments of their courses, and these need to be further developed.

Helping students to develop graphical literacy can be akin to creative writing as a creative experience. Students should be encouraged to use graphing in all types of written communication and in study.

Finally, if graphing is to be included in the curriculum of reading, English, and most other subjects to a greater extent, it needs to be more highly valued. Some techniques for showing greater value for graphical literacy include graphing assignments and greater recognition on the part of teachers of the communication value of graphs.

References

Fry, Edward. *Graphical Comprehension.* Providence: R.I.: Jamestown Publishers, 1981.

Levin, Joel R. "What Have We Learned about Maximizing What Children Learn?" In *Cognitive Learning in Children: Theories and Strategies,* edited by J.R. Levin and V.L. Allen. New York, N.Y.: Academic Press, 1976.

Paivio, A. "Language and Knowledge of the World." *Educational Researcher,* vol. 3 (1974), pp. 5-12.

Singer, Harry and Dan Donlan. *Learning from Text.* Boston, Mass.: Little, Brown, 1980.

Whittrock, Merl C. "The Cognitive Movement in Instruction." *Educational Psychologist,* vol. 13 (1978), pp. 15-29.

A Taxonomy of Graphs by Edward Fry

Too often, if you ask people what a graph is, they will tell you about only two or three kinds, such as a bar graph (contrasting two or more quantitative amounts) or a pie graph (showing percentages). The taxonomy presented here both defines and broadens the term "graph." It attempts to show what is and what is not considered a graph. With five major categories and a number of subcategories, it attempts to expand the thinking of students and teachers about the kinds of information a graph can communicate. It is interesting that four of the five major categories of this Taxonomy of Graphs are not mathematical or, more accurately, not quantitative. By calling such diverse things as time lines, maps, and abstract drawings "graphs," the Taxonomy attempts to expand the notion of "graphness."

Perhaps a definition of a graph is in order. *A graph is a two-dimensional visual representation of a concept in nonverbal or at most partly verbal form.* A graph may use words, numbers, or symbols, but a major portion of the information communicated must be by line, image, or area. It is more globally visual than detailed symbolic and sequential. A graph tends to show "the big picture" or gestalt, with greater or lesser amounts of supporting detail. Often interrelationships can be seen better with a graph than with a purely verbal or numerical presentation.

Just because a graph may be basically nonverbal or nonsymbolic does not mean that it is "culture free." Students must acquire the ability to comprehend and create graphs either by direct instruction or incidental learning. It is the major point of the accompanying article that graphical literacy, the ability to read and write graphs, should be taught in school.

Uses of the Taxonomy

The Taxonomy of Graphs can be used as the basis for curriculum development. Keep in mind that taxonomies are not necessarily hierarchical. A teacher or textbook author can develop lessons in each of the major areas, in whatever order best matches the subject matter. For example, social studies teachers can express and explain the history of any event with a time line, while a physical education teacher outlines a basketball tournament with a hierarchy graph. A vocational teacher might like to give directions by means of a process chart instead of a written paragraph, and a science teacher would be hard put to explain electronic circuitry or the operation of a copper smelter without a flow chart. Similar examples could be derived for the Quantitative, Spacial, Pictorial, and Hypothetical areas of the Taxonomy.

The reading teacher, of course, must help students to read and comprehend in all of these areas. The reading teacher is also sometimes responsible for some writing instruction, so it is important to teach the expression of ideas in *all* (not just some) of the Taxonomy's categories. Even if the reading teacher does not teach writing, the teaching of "study skills" is often an important part of the reading curriculum.

Study skills instruction should include not just the reading and writing of graphs, but the fact that a prime study technique is to translate a verbal passage into a graph. This alone is the basis of many interesting lessons.

A taxonomy such as this has another important curriculum-related function. It can serve as the basis of achievement tests. For better or worse, today's students are tested many times. They take reading readiness tests (which are incidentally often highly graphic), achievement tests given by the school district, state or province-wide achievement tests, college entrance tests, civil service or employment tests, etc. Often these tests include graphs. What kind of graphs? This Taxonomy can extend the range, or suggest various types of graphs that can be included in tests.

The Taxonomy might be useful to students and practitioners in various fields outside of education, such as advertising, journalism, television, computer programming, business report writing, or in any case where someone receives or sends two-dimensional visual information.

Finally, the Taxonomy of Graphs might enhance teacher education so that teachers will more regularly and systematically employ graphs as a basic form of communication. Most teachers use some graphs in expressing ideas. The Taxonomy is saying, use more and use a greater variety.

Levels of Graph Use

To paraphrase Jerome Bruner: Nearly any type of graph can be taught at any level if it is properly done.

Kindergarten is not a day too early to teach picture comprehension or simplified map reading. In fact, students may arrive at school with all but too much practice in interpreting the semipictorial graphs that dominate Saturday morning TV. Numbers are certainly made more real with line and bar graph explanations, and even some fairly abstract ideas can be communicated with boxes and connecting arrows.

At the other end of the education curriculum, subjects like computer science, epistemology, and architecture use a high level of graphing. In between, at every grade and in every single subject, graphs are an effective communication medium.

In brief, graphical literacy, the reading and writing of graphs, should be taught at every level from preschool through graduate school. As a separate subject in the reading curriculum, I would expect that the most emphasis would be in upper elementary and middle schools.

PROGRAM DEVELOPMENT

From assessment to instructional strategies to materials to skills—this is the developmental sequence of a reading program, but not the entire story. In each case, the program to emerge will display uniqueness according to the range of variables made possible by the vicissitudes, talents, and demands of particular teachers in particular content areas in particular teaching situations. No two teachers will assess their students' need in the same way (even those teaching the same content at the same grade level). They will not determine instructional strategies from the same perspective, nor select materials, nor teach skills in the same manner.

Yet there is more to program development than this necessary and desirable diversity. A reading program, whether one developed by an individual teacher in a single classroom or one implemented at the state or provincial level, is always greater than the sum of its parts. Although programs will share characteristics of assessment, strategies, materials, and skills, the result of combining these components will always exceed in scope and variety what could be predicted by examining the components in isolation.

The articles in this section exemplify this point from varying perspectives. Perhaps a subtitle to the section could be "The People, The Process, and The Product." Certainly, the people involved in program development represent a vital resource if allowed the time and opportunity to develop into a mutually supportive and clearly focused team of professionals. The article by Anders discusses how this can be done through providing guidance in the establishment of school reading committees and gives suggestions as to how these committees can function. In the second article,

Cottier and Koehler carry this theme further in their description of a study skills program involving the cooperative efforts of content area teachers, reading specialists, and parents. Process is considered in articles by Frankel and Shenkman, respectively. In Frankel's article (one which also appeared in the first edition of this book), the process of developing a student centered classroom reading program is described from the point of view of the social studies teacher who did it. Shenkman, on the other hand, addresses process from the perspective of the learner, and in so doing reassesses the notion of behavioral objectives and their implications for reading instruction in terms of recent research in psycholinguistics. It seems that, while objectives are never out of place in program development, the nature and focus of these objectives have shifted from eliciting students' overt responses to test type questions to creating learning situations which facilitate students' covert responses to the print material before them. The product of these responses, at least to the extent that it can be embodied in program design, is the concern of Vacca and Vacca in the last article. Here the question of competency is addressed in a balanced and thoughtful argument for functionality in program development.

- *What five reasons are given for forming a reading committee?*
- *What are the functions of the reading committee?*

DREAM OF A SECONDARY READING PROGRAM? PEOPLE ARE THE KEY

Patricia L. Anders
University of Arizona

Secondary reading specialists often dream of developing an all-school reading program, a reading program in which the content area teachers and the reading specialist work together to facilitate all students' reading development. For at least two reasons, however, this dream is difficult to achieve.

First, many reading specialists are at a loss as to how to begin and carry out such a program. Their education has emphasized how to teach reading, but not the processes that are involved in learning through reading. The emphasis of any content-based reading program must be on the latter. Second, many classroom teachers either know very little about content-area-based reading programs and therefore lack experiences that support the efficacy of this type of program, or strongly believe that secondary reading programs are primarily remedial in nature and that it is the reading teacher's responsibility to teach all those "problem readers." These two obstacles often discourage even the most enthusiastic and well meaning reading specialist.

However, both problems can be solved by extending and modifying a notion suggested by Sargent (1969). Sargent advocated the creation of a reading committee representative of each content area within a school. She reports that the "prime purposes of the committee should be to identify the specific needs within each department (relative to the utilization of skills by students) and decide how best to meet these needs. This committee should also receive communications relative to the needs and wishes of teachers in each department regarding their knowledge of reading and their ability to incorporate the use of reading skills into the mastery of their specific content areas" (p. 19).

Adapted from *Journal of Reading,* January 1981, *24,* 316-320.

These points are well made, but they need to be developed further. A reading committee (sometimes called a council) can be the most powerful tool a reading specialist has in developing a content-area-based reading program. The reading committee opens both classroom doors and content area teachers' minds to the concept of an all-school, content-area-based, developmental secondary reading program. This article provides a rationale for the reading committee, poses alternative methods for establishing a reading committee and finally suggests ways the reading committee can promote reading in the content areas.

Why a Reading Committee?

There are at least five justifications for having a reading committee in the secondary school.

First, in the committee, working relationships between faculty members and the reading specialist are developed in a natural and efficient context. Without the structure of the committee, it may take semesters or even years to develop those relationships. Within the committee structure, it is possible for the specialist and teachers to exchange ideas and gain respect for each other.

Second, the reading committee provides a forum for the reading specialist to receive feedback both on the practicality, acceptability, and efficacy of new ideas for the reading program and on the success, mediocrity, or failure of ideas already carried out.

Third, committee members can serve as "door openers" to their respective departments. Teachers may be more willing to listen to a department member than to an outsider, especially an outsider who is a "specialist." For example, opportunities will exist for the committee member and the specialist to make team presentations at department meetings and inservice programs.

Fourth, the reading specialist who has limited experience and knowledge in content area reading can learn from and with the content area teachers who are serving on the committee. The specialist can share knowledge about the reading process, and the committee members can share knowledge about the processes involved in learning content area concepts. Together they can learn how to facilitate the reading of subject related materials.

Fifth, and perhaps most important, responsibility for the all-school reading program is put where it belongs: on the shoulders of both content area teachers and the reading specialist. This is important for two reasons. When teachers share responsibility for the program, they are much less likely to use the reading specialist as a scapegoat for reading problems. Second, the ideas generated from a group of committed people are far more likely to be valid, workable, and carried out than those of just one person.

These five points are good reasons for at least trying a reading committee. The next logical question is how does one begin?

Forming the Committee

The committee may be formed by volunteers, by election, by appointment, or by some combination of these three. The decision on how to form the committee is important because the initial success of the committee may rest upon the method chosen for its formation. The entire faculty will be watching this process and will judge the specialist's actions. If the faculty believes that the specialist has considered their opinions in setting up the committee, the reading specialist will have taken a step toward winning their trust and confidence.

Factors a reading specialist should consider are: (1) What is the customary procedure (volunteers, election, appointment) in my school for forming such committees? (2) Which method will give the committee a high status in the school? (3) Which method does the school principal prefer? (4) Which method do the teachers prefer?

The Figure shows a grid that facilitates this important decision-making process. By quantifying their own perceptions of each of the factors in relation to each of the methods, reading specialists can determine the method most appropriate for a particular school. If all factors are not equal, the more important one should be weighted proportionately. The specialist will have to rely on intuition in this matter.

Example of Use of Decision-Making Grid

Method	Volunteer	Elected	Appointed	Combination
Factors				
Precedence	+1	0	+1	0
Status	-1	+1	+1	+1
Principal	+1	-1	+1	0
Teacher	+1	+1	0	+1
Sum	+2	+1	+3	+2

+1 = positive reactions
0 = does not matter, is irrelevant, or specialist is unsure
-1 = negative reactions

The Figure shows how one specialist perceived the answers to each of the factors in terms of each possible method. By summing each column, it was possible to estimate which method was the most appropriate for her school. The decision that was made was to encourage teachers to let the principal or specialist know of their interest in being on the committee and then for the reading specialist and principal to invite one faculty member from each department to join the committee. The specialist and principal appointed all teachers who expressed interest and then invited the remaining members according to two criteria: (1) Faculty members were invited who the principal thought were perceived by their colleagues as being very good teachers; (2) Faculty members were invited who served often in leadership positions within their departments. Two people volunteered, each from different departments; therefore, one person from each of the other departments was appointed. All appointed faculty members agreed to serve on the committee. No department heads were invited to join the committee because they, as a group, could work with the reading specialist through department head meetings. Sargent (1969) advocates a heterogeneous committee of the reading specialist's choosing. This is not a bad idea, but may not always be appropriate.

Functions and Responsibilities

Each secondary school's reading committee operates a little differently, but here are some ideas that have been successful in many schools.

One idea is to turn the first several meetings of the committee into an intensive inservice program. A specialist may share ideas about materials, evaluation and development, about teaching vocabulary and study skills, or about other introductory concepts.

Another idea is to give the committee members readings from professional publications that deal with the incorporation of reading instruction into each member's content area. These readings could be a basis for discussion and possibly team teaching opportunities.

An outgrowth of the readings mentioned above could be the creation of a "Reading in the Content Areas" handbook. One reading committee put together loose-leaf notebooks for each teacher. These contained professional articles, followed by activities and lesson plans that had been developed by the school's teachers. Teachers appreciated seeing each other's work. Eventually, this handbook was distributed district-wide.

A third idea is to have the reading committee set up yearly goals for the all-school reading program. Examples of specific goals include (1) encouraging faculty members' personal reading by starting a paperback book exchange in the faculty lounge or cafeteria, (2) carrying out inservice for the entire faculty, (3) creating a "project vocabulary" (i.e., teachers decide upon the most important conceptual vocabulary in their content areas and devise various means to insure that all students understand those words in relation to that subject), and (4) establishing a schoolwide sustained silent reading program (McCracken, 1971).

A fourth responsibility of a reading committee might be to establish a network of tutors trained by the reading committee to work with students in classrooms, resource centers, or a reading lab.

A fifth idea is to arrange opportunities for a committee member to invite departmental colleagues along on visitations to schools that are success-fully incorporating reading into the content area. This idea worked particu-larly well, for example, when substitutes were provided by the school so that the reading specialist, the industrial arts committee member, and an industrial arts teacher could visit an innovative industrial arts department about 100 miles away. The industrial arts teacher, who had been the least cooperative teacher in terms of the reading program, became one of the reading program's greatest advocates.

Another idea is to create a reading newsletter. One school called its newsletter "From the Reading Lady" and published it bimonthly. Each committee member regularly contributed articles. For example, the librar-ian reviewed books of interest to the faculty and a biology teacher shared a system of notetaking that she had developed. The high school printing class duplicated the newsletter, and it was distributed to each member of the school staff, to the central office, to the principals and reading teachers in other districts and nearby schools, and to the local university. The newslet-ter was acclaimed by many, and the reading specialist observed that it served as a catalyst for the involvement of teachers in the reading program.

A final important responsibility of the reading committee may be to pro-vide input on how to spend the reading specialist's budget. The specialist might look for multilevel content area materials and share those materials with the committee members. The committee members can alert the spe-cialist to materials that would be appropriate for their respective depart-ments. Purchased materials would be turned over to the appropriate departments, with suggestions for use from the specialist and a reading committee member.

Each of these responsibilities and functions of the reading committee will vary with every school depending upon the needs of the school, the available resources, and the creativity of the reading specialist and the reading committee. However, these ideas should provide seeds for other ideas that will make an all-school reading program a reality. A content area reading program will succeed if teachers are given an opportunity to be responsible for it.

References

McCracken, Robert A. "Initiating Sustained Silent Reading." *Journal of Reading,* vol. 14 (May 1971) pp. 521-24, 582-83.

Sargent, Eileen. "Integrating Reading Skills in the Content Areas." In *Fusing Reading Skills and Content,* edited by H. Alan Robinson and Ellen Lamar Thomas. Newark, Del.: International Reading Association, 1969.

Anders

- *What is the role of the content area teacher described in this program?*
- *How could different study skills required for learning in different content areas be incorporated into a program such as this one?*

A STUDY SKILLS UNIT FOR JUNIOR HIGH STUDENTS

Susan J. Cottier
Sheri Koehler Bauman
Lesher Junior High School
Fort Collins, Colorado

Content area teachers often assume that the study skills necessary for successful performance at the secondary level have been acquired by students in elementary school, in the reading lab, or via incidental learning. On the other hand, parents often express the feeling that their children lack efficient study habits and tools.

To answer parent inquiries about ways to help children at home and to refute or support assumptions regarding our students' study skills, we attempted to determine the degree to which students in our junior high school had mastered study skills and to design an effective program to meet their needs. We devised a survey instrument to assess how well these students took and used notes, used the organizational patterns of a written selection, and prepared for tests, and whether they were aware of test taking strategies.

Ninth grade social studies students served as the pilot group for the survey because the social studies course was required of all students and therefore provided a cross section of ability and achievement levels. In addition, these somewhat older students' experience would have afforded them the opportunity to develop these skills, if indeed they do develop without direct instruction.

Responses to the survey instrument showed clearly that study skills, particularly notetaking and awareness of patterns of organization, had not been acquired. Even students who produced copious notes included few if any abbreviations and showed no evidence of having any particular structure or system of notetaking.

Adapted from *Journal of Reading,* April 1978, *21,* 626-630.

On a questionnaire distributed to teachers of all subjects and grade levels in the junior high school, teachers indicated whether they expected students to take notes during class discussions and lectures, films, and from texts; what kinds of tests they used; and whether independent reading in the textbook was assigned. Nearly unanimous in their responses, teachers expected students to take notes in class and during films and other media presentations. The majority used short answer tests, composed mainly of sentence completion and matching items.

Acting on the results of our survey which showed students' lack of mastery of study skills, we designed a program in which ninth grade social studies students and seventh grade developmental reading classes received instruction in study and notetaking skills and in which specific suggestions for home study were offered to parents at an evening session. The seventh grade classes were taught by the reading teacher while the ninth grade classes were taught with a team approach, with the learning disabilities and reading specialists making presentations which were monitored and followed up by the social studies teacher.

The team approach appeared to be far more effective. The seventh graders did not seem to transfer the skills to other areas, which could be due in part to their maturity level but was due to some extent to the isolated way in which the program was presented. The direct follow-up made possible by the social studies member of the team seemed influential in helping the students see the value of the skills.

Parent Involvement

At an evening session for parents, we described the program to them and explained and illustrated the system of notetaking we were using, emphasizing the purpose and advantages of the recall column. We suggested that parents encourage their children to take notes in class and review them at home in the evening. The overlapping technique for studying was demonstrated and recommended.

Suggestions for productive home study were offered. Good lighting, quiet place, frequent short sessions, scheduling of time, etc., were discussed. Patterns of organization were presented and their relationship to good notetaking shown.

Response to the parent session was extremely positive, with many parents expressing a desire to see the program incorporated throughout the school.

The study skills program which is described in detail below was modified and added to on the basis of the pilot program. In planning the program, Walter Pauk's book *How to Study in College* (1974) and personal correspondence proved invaluable.

The unit requires seven classroom periods scheduled throughout the quarter. The flexible schedule allows follow-up time for the content teachers and time for most students to master one skill before progressing to the next. Presentations were made by the learning disabilities specialist and the reading specialist, with the content teacher present.

First session. The first session is designed to make students aware of how valuable study skills can be. *American Study Habits Survey* (American Guidance Service 1964) is distributed so students can evaluate their knowledge of good study habits. Students will reevaluate themselves at the end of the course.

In order to demonstrate how organization aids learning, several activities are undertaken. In one activity, the class is randomly divided into three groups. The first group receives a list of nonsense syllables; the second group, 10 words randomly chosen; the third, a list of 10 words in an order that forms a logical sentence. The groups are given one minute to study their lists and then are asked to write the list from memory.

The difference in performance among the groups is obvious. When the contents of the three lists are revealed, the reason for the success of the third group becomes evident. The class should reach the conclusion that the third list was easiest to learn because the material was organized in a meaningful way.

In a similar activity, two groups can attempt to memorize lists of nonsense syllables, one of which is alphabetically arranged while the other is not. Students should realize that those who learned the alphabetical list did so as a result of the way in which it was organized.

Another activity is one in which students are shown a lengthy list of items such as TV programs, supermarket products, book titles, headlines, etc., and are given an opportunity to discuss possible organizational schemes. [All of the activities mentioned above are found in *Making Sense* (1975) by Christian Gerhard.]

During the remainder of the first week, the content area teacher emphasizes categorizing and organizing activities using the content material. For example, students could classify the words on one page of the index or glossary of their text by establishing general categories under which the items could be grouped.

Second session. Notetaking procedure is presented during the second session. After reviewing many notetaking techniques, we chose for this course the Cornell System, developed by Walter Pauk. Students reread the notes they have taken and extract key words to be added to a recall column. Basically, students review and edit their notes and synthesize main ideas.

Have students use a piece of paper divided vertically into two columns. The column on the left is the recall column; the rest of the page is used for taking the notes. While the content teacher presents a short lesson, students take notes and the specialist team takes notes on transparencies. After the lesson, their notes are projected for the class, and the group selects key words for the recall column. Students can compare their efforts with the teachers' sample.

Subsequently, the content teacher begins lessons by projecting a page with the note column covered, reviewing the terms in the recall column, and showing how key words should be used to trigger recall of concepts, definitions, or facts. As a method of self-checking, uncover the note column. This model can be followed by the student in home study. The content teacher should present short lessons to allow time for practicing and reviewing notetaking. Some students could take their notes on a transparency to provide a model for their classmates.

Third session. The third lesson uses samples from student notes to point out the advantages of abbreviation and other time-saving techniques, such as boxing, underlining new vocabulary, color coding different types of information, and highlighting. (See pp. 136-39 of Pauk's book for a list of abbreviations.)

For practice, give the class a page of notes to be improved by abbreviating, highlighting, or any other appropriate technique. Let them edit and discuss other samples.

Content teachers must follow up notetaking skills in some manner each day. Students found comparing their notes with those of others, sharing lists of key words, and discussing organization of notes to be valuable. Above all, content teachers must never assume that students are automatically taking meaningful notes at this point. Notetaking is habit which requires guidance to develop efficiently over a period of time.

Fourth session. The fourth session is devoted to recognizing common organizational patterns of expository material. An examination of the textual material used in our school indicated that the following patterns were most common and best suited for notetaking: cause and effect, enumeration, comparison and contrast, and chronological order. Explain these patterns as students examine samples of each; develop signal words for each organizational pattern. (Examples: cause and effect—*because, therefore;* enumeration—*first, next, finally;* comparison and contrast—*however, nevertheless;* chronological order—*after, then,* etc.)

Give students an opportunity to practice identifying organizational patterns and taking notes. They should use their course textbook whenever possible. Ask students to find paragraphs in their reading that illustrate the different patterns and to point out examples in films, newspaper articles, and so forth.

Fifth session. This session is based on a mock test which makes clear through exaggeration how knowledge of test-taking strategies can improve one's score. Include these types of items: multiple-choice questions with illogical distractors; true/false items with absolute terms such as always and never; completion items that demand certain grammatical categories (e.g., use of "an" to signal an answer that begins with a vowel); matching exercises in which the process of elimination is a factor; and questions whose answers are planted within other questions. After students have taken the test, allow them to discuss these test taking techniques and others, such as choosing questions when an option is available, budgeting time during a test, changing answers, guessing, etc.

Sixth session. Schedule session six for a time when a test is pending. Demonstrate how lapping the pages of notes one over another presents a list of key terms. By uncovering the note column, the student can instantly review and reinforce information. Other techniques for studying, such as flash cards, mastering spelling lists and time lines, etc., are explained using material which will be on the test so the period doubles as a study session. A discussion of good study habits is valuable at this point, perhaps referring to the inventory used on the first day.

Seventh session. The final session is devoted to illustrating how the organizational patterns studied can be used in planning written assignments, particularly responses on essay tests. At this time, students may retake the *Study Habits Survey* and notice their improved scores. Let students evaluate the course, as they will surely have some good suggestions and comments.

The success of the study skills program is dependent on parent involvement, the integration of study skills and content, and consistent follow-up of skills sessions by the content teachers. The difference between "A" and "C" students may not be intelligence or even motivation, but may be how well they have mastered efficient study skills as they progress through school.

References

American Guidance Service. *American Study Habits Survey.* Circle Pines, Minn.: American Guidance Service, 1964.

Gerhard, Christian. *Making Sense: Reading Comprehension Improved through Categorizing.* Newark, Del.: International Reading Association, 1975.

Pauk, Walter. *How to Study in College.* Boston, Mass.: Houghton Mifflin Company, 1974.

- *What are the five specific activities outlined?*
- *How does each activity contribute to students' learning through reading?*

READING SKILLS THROUGH SOCIAL STUDIES CONTENT AND STUDENT INVOLVEMENT

Jill Frankel Hauser
LearningWorks
Redding, California

Within the four walls of the social studies classroom sat, stretched, laughed, and yawned thirty-eight seventh graders. According to standardized tests, their reading levels ranged from grades three through eleven. Interests varied to include the gamut: who was going with whom in the class, the fate of the American Indian, and Kung Fu. This diverse group was met with one sturdy seventh grade history text and a classroom library untouched by teenaged hands.

To meet the needs of this diverse group, I coupled social studies content with critical reading and communication skills. I expanded my definition of reading to mean not merely the ability to decode the printed word, but the ability to understand and evaluate all forms of primary and secondary resources. Reading would also include the ability to apply the comprehended information through a variety of media from the printed word, to graphics, to dramatics. I developed multilevel lessons with enough flexibility for each student to grasp the content at his own level of reading ability from remedial to gifted. I also designed involvement and success into each unit to meet the affective goal of having each student develop positive feelings toward himself. To put this theory into practical classroom use, I developed five approaches calling for total student involvement.

Homemade Library

During the first week of class, I disposed of most of the library and presented the class with an unusual sight—an empty bookcase. "This is our library. What are you going to do about it?"

Adapted from *Journal of Reading*, October 1974, *18*, 23-26.

(Silence).

"You are going to write your own books."

"Us write books? You're crazy! That's impossible."

Somehow the notion of writing a book is very monumental. But the paper was turned sideways and stapled through the middle, and our library grew.

We used a language experience approach and allowed total freedom in terms of subject matter and language structure. The results were highly individual. Some books were simple, others were lavishly illustrated and could be officially "checked out" by signing the included card. The more advanced readers researched a topic from encyclopedias and books. Others wrote love stories or events inspired from their own lives or television. Those who could write only a few sentences wrote captions for pictures in their scrapbooks. Because the class was heterogenous, I assigned student tutors to help other students with writing, grammar, or oral reading of their books. Students often reported on each other's books for book reports, a great honor for the authors. To this basic core of student-made books, I added catalogues, magazines, and appropriate paperbacks. Our library was now used.

A geography unit on map reading skills made our classroom look like a game factory. I put the responsibility on the students for producing a library of social studies games. Each student brought a road map to class. They began by writing and answering questions about the map. Questions involved all aspects of map reading from mileage scales to identifying interstate highways to being able to determine populations of cities.

The next job was to turn the map into a game board. Each student marked a route on the map from one city to another which represented the route from starting point to finishing point of the game. Cities along the way indicated stops. Players moved from city to city based on their ability to answer map skills questions. These questions were written on cards with questions on one side and answers on the back. To complete the package, instructions were included on how to play the game.

Students reinforced map and reading skills in designing and playing their games. Instruction writing proved to be an excellent communications assignment. Playing games with a friend was a popular activity.

The success of student made games led me to use the approach for a combined values, social studies, and reading project later in the year. I assigned the project as follows: Students could choose any social studies topic to work with. They were required to write a question and answer booklet incorporating the results of their research. A game board, experimental in its form of graphic communication, would indicate the students's values and written instructions would tell how to play the game.

For example, the boys who designed the game "All Junkies are Dopes" put a positive value on not using drugs. This then was the goal and finish of the game. Along the route to a drug-free life, however, a player might land on a square saying, "Busted for marijuana possession. Go back five spaces." Other squares required the player to know the answer to a question about drugs, found in the question booklet, before advancing.

A wide range of values was encouraged. "You and Me: The Marriage Game" made getting married the end goal. The researched questions included facts about international customs of marriage. In the "Women's Liberation Game" a player would win when she attained her equal rights before the law. In this game getting married might move a player back! Here research centered around the Equal Rights Amendment.

This was a multilevel assignment. While the "Watergate Game" required comprehensive reading and research skills and using magazines and newspapers, the "Survival Game—the Game of Gangs" involved simple recording of one's own knowledge of the neighborhood

Students read enthusiastically about their topics and employed critical thinking skills in formulating their questions. Students playing each other's games needed to read instruction booklets in order to play, encouraging students to communicate clearly and players to read accurately. Students made value judgments based on conclusions derived from their research.

Consumer education was our next problem. As a springboard I gave each student copies of food labels. I asked students to critically read the labels and identify the unnecessary or misleading information. Using the inquiry approach, we compiled a list of facts we felt were necessary for the consumer to know when buying a food item (weight, ingredients, price, and so forth).

I had students apply what they had learned by designing two can labels. One can would be the ideal can and the other, the imperfect can. The labels were drawn on paper strips, then rolled and stapled to look like real cans. For example, "Friskies" was priced at 20 cents per can and contained meat by-products, while "Riskies" was priced at two cans for 53 cents and contained cereal.

The next part of the unit involved team work. I divided the students into small firms whose function it was to market one item. The conditions: 1) There must indeed be a market for the item within the school community. 2) The item must not have an adverse effect on the environment.

Condition one was satisfied through marketing research. For example, would the bicycle firm have greater success selling a three-speed, five-speed, or ten-speed bike? Students compiled a list of questions relevant to their products. The questions became part of a group questionnaire used to poll their schoolmates during lunch break. In this way the most popular model of television, motorcycle, car, or even bug spray could be determined.

Condition two was satisfied by writing an environmental impact study of the product. Little information was available on this topic so each firm cooperatively wrote how they ideally would want their product to affect the environment. Students became aware that a firm had a greater responsibility to the public than merely selling a popular product.

Communication was my emphasis as students designed ads for their products. We discussed real magazine ads in terms of their effectiveness in selling the product and not violating consumer rights. Students designed magazine ads for their products, illustrating them and using persuasive writing techniques. That night's homework was to watch and analyze television commercials. This brought us into a discussion on mass media and led each firm to dramatize commercials for their own products. The class evaluated the resulting commercials according to the standards they had determined.

The climactic ending to this unit was two neighborhood field trips. We visited a billboard manufacturing company and Lawry's Foods headquarters. Students voluntarily brought lists of questions and thoroughly quizzed the guides. One student even brought a tape recorder so we could further analyze all we had learned back in the classroom laboratory. This approach to consumer education brought reading and social studies into a real world context for the students.

Drama Use

Drama was a multipurpose classroom tool. It brought us together as a class. It allowed some class members to succeed where they had never done so before. It allowed students to communicate through a new medium and practice their speech and language skills. Values were examined through drama with role playing activities. I gave the students a situation, they improvised the rest: You are being asked to join a gang. How will you and the gang members respond? Action. You are taking a test. Your best friend signals you for some answers. What do you do? Action. In the middle of the action I might ask the actors to switch roles to see the situation from the opposite viewpoint. I participated, often taking the role of student, and had students play my role as teacher, parent, or friend. Students were soon bringing in their own real or created situations to act out. Improvising their reactions, students examined their own behavior and that of their peers in a realistic setting. The popularity of this activity made it a reward for good work during the rest of the week.

Values were also considered in our social studies content areas. In a unit on the penal system, drama was used as a values monitor and a feedback system for me to determine what had been learned. After reading an article on prisons, students discussed their feelings in groups. They reported back to class their conceptions of the ideal penal system by acting out the life of a prisoner in this setting. This sort of approach to subject matter resulted in a high degree of student interaction and involvement.

On the last day of school students took home their original books and games. Here were tangible results of the achievement they had made during the year and some good review material to use over the summer to polish up on reading and social studies skills. And most students went home with some very positive feelings about themselves, too!

- *What dangers are identified in using behavioral objectives in program development?*
- *What is the difference between behavioral objectives and behavioral processes?*

BEYOND BEHAVIORAL OBJECTIVES:
BEHAVIORAL PROCESSES

Harriet Shenkman
Bronx Community College

The introduction of behavioral objectives into reading programs has been welcomed, lauded, and glorified by some, and dismissed, denounced, and lambasted by others. Proponents proclaim the usefulness of behavioral objectives in clarifying and organizing what is to be taught, in facilitating the measurement of improvement, and in explicating standards for the purposes of evaluation and accountability. Opponents denounce the use of behavioral objectives, claiming that they are restricted to trivial outcomes and ignore higher-order goals such as the actualization of human potential. Furthermore, they claim, behavioral objectives are insensitive to internal change unlikely to be revealed by overt behavior and tend to foster rigidity, discouraging the examination of consequences and the generation of alternatives. The arguments of both opponents and proponents are justifiable from different perspectives.

A real danger does exist that once behavioral objectives are formulated in a program, they will become fixed and rigid. A reading program may, consequently, become impaled on the spikes of behavioral objectives, shifting its focus from instructional process to management routines. Objectives are selected, unanalyzed, from a laundry list of reading skills and are easily justified because remedial students need almost all skills. Preassessment and postassessment are determined on the basis of selected objectives and prescriptive routines are focused upon.

The instructor becomes absorbed in measuring the selected skills, assigning exercises, remeasuring the same skills and keeping charts, graphs, and other records. S/he believes that his/her instructional duty has been satisfied once s/he has "covered" all the objectives and completed the

Adapted from *Journal of Reading,* November 1978, 22, 113-116.

record keeping procedures. In effect, the educational program becomes metamorphosed into a training system.

Objectives as Catalysts

On the other hand, the possibility exists of formulating behavioral objectives in such a way that they serve as a catalyst for more dynamic reading instruction. The process must, however, be viewed as a liberally constructed empirical method (Zais 1976). Objectives are formulated in an open-ended fashion with the realization that they are only behavioral clues hypothesized as probable signs of learning. This contrasts to a dogmatic application of operational methods following a strict notion of ends as terminal points around which a fixed program is built. Instead, encouragement is given to constant examination of the reality and consequences of objectives following Dewey's definition (1964) of ends as "redirecting pivots" in a constant flow of action.

Current reading skills programs, if founded upon liberally constructed instructional objectives, will be able to go beyond objectives as commonly formulated when new information warrants change. In particular, today, reading skills objectives need to be reevaluated in light of psycholinguistic information and about the processes underlying reading performance. As pointed out by Morris (1977), who is attempting to formulate test domains in writing based on information processing models, the usefulness of domain referenced tests depends ultimately on the details and well-foundedness of the model of concepts, behaviors, and knowledge upon which they are based. This observation is relevant to the behavioral objectives upon which tests in reading are founded, which have tended to become fixed on inadequate and outdated models of what constitutes reading.

For example, typical behavioral objectives in the area of reading comprehension are:

1. Given a 10th grade level paragraph, the student will be able to write the main idea of the paragraph.
2. Given a 10th grade level paragraph, the student will be able to write logical inferences from the information found in the paragraph.

These objectives tell nothing about the complex processes involved in reaching the terminal behaviors of deriving the main idea or logical inference. Because they do not illuminate what a reader does during the act of reading, they are not useful in developing instructional methods. In fact, objectives of this type are useful only as a guide for constructing reading comprehension questions. Instruction which consists primarily of paragraphs and such terminal exercise questions may result in higher scores on similarly constructed tests but are limited in developing the cognitive and linguistic strategies that produce fluent readers and transfer to daily reading behaviors.

Add Psycholinguistic Strategies

The psycholinguistic knowledge that objectives should encompass is summarized below from a description by Cooper and Petrosky (1976) of the strategies that a skilled reader uses to process print.

1. The skilled reader discovers the distinctive features in letters, words, and meanings.
2. S/he takes chances in order to learn about the text and to predict meaning.
3. S/he reads to identify meaning rather than letters or words.
4. S/he guesses from context at unfamiliar words or skips them.
5. S/he actively brings his/her knowledge of the world and of the topic in the text to the print.
6. S/he reads as though s/he expects the text to make sense.
7. S/he makes use of orthographic, syntactic, and semantic redundancy to arrive at meaning.
8. S/he maintains enough speed to overcome the limitations of the visual processing and memory systems.

In addition, models are currently being developed of how meaning is represented in semantic memory and how entire units of text are processed (Kintsch, 1974, 1976). This research should generate additions to our list of even more sophisticated psychological operations performed in the act of reading. For example, Kintsch postulates that a reader goes through the mental operations of deletion, generalization and construction to arrive at the gist of a paragraph.

One way of incorporating psycholinguistic strategies into a reading program is to include objectives in which the student demonstrates her/his use of strategies by answering specially designed questions posed by the instructor immediately after having read a paragraph or longer selection. For example:

> After reading a paragraph on the 10th grade reading level, the student will be able to answer questions posed by the instructor which demonstrate that s/he has attended to the distinctive features of the meaning of an unfamiliar word.

The particular questions asked would depend upon the specific paragraph and word and the instructor's understanding of the role of distinctive features. As an illustration, the student reads a paragraph which contains the following sentence:

> She realized he was a philanderer when she encountered him three times in one week with different female companions.

The following key questions and probe questions are asked by the instructor:

1. Can you rephrase this sentence in your own words? Did you guess at the meaning of the word "philanderer"?
2. What can you tell about how the word is used in this sentence? Does it serve as an action word, a person, place, or thing, etc.?
3. Can the word represent only a particular type of person? What items in the sentence or paragraph delimit the type of person this word stands for?

The key questions let us know if the student is using relevant psycholinguistic strategies such as guessing and looking for distinctive semantic and syntactic features. The probe questions, asked after answers to key questions have been given, show whether s/he is focusing on the most productive features. If the reader is not making optimum use of appropriate mental operations, the questions serve to guide her/him in becoming aware of their use. We are not interested here in whether s/he can recite the definition of the word.

A second example of an objective and questions based on psycholinguistic insights is related to the psychological operations involved in processing entire units of text.

> After reading a paragraph on the 10th grade reading level, the student will be able to answer questions posed by the instructor which demonstrate that s/he has used the summarizing operations of deletion, generalization and construction to arrive at the main idea or gist of the paragraph.

Questions posed by the instructor might be:

1. Can you summarize the paragraph in one sentence?
2. How did you arrive at this summary? How does the second sentence relate to your summary? the third sentence? (And so forth.)

A paragraph is selected which illustrates how the various ideas in the paragraph are deleted, generalized and constructed to arrive at a summary or main idea.

Teacher as Analyst

Questioning techniques such as the one described could be used on a day-to-day instructional basis and could be incorporated into a diagnostic or testing situation where the students read a selection silently and provide written or oral answers to the instructor's questions. The focus is upon the reading process instead of upon terminal behaviors. It is consonant with the role of the teacher advocated by Smith (1975), namely, the teacher as a person who is cognizant of the internal processes underlying the reading and uses her/his knowledge to facilitate reader development rather than supply artificial tasks which impede it.

When the instructional framework of a reading program is built upon an adequate model of the reading process, the instructor's sensitivity is heightened and his/her role is transformed from managerial to analytic. The reading program itself grows beyond behavioral objectives into a sophisticated program of diagnosis and remediation based on behavioral processes.

References

Cooper, Charles R. and Anthony R. Petrosky. "A Psycholinguistic View of the Fluent Reading Process." *Journal of Reading,* vol. 20, no. 3 (December 1976). pp. 184-207.

Dewey, John. *John Dewey on Education: Selected Writings.* Reginald D. Archambault, Ed. New York, N.Y.: Random House, 1964.

Goodman, Kenneth S. and James T. Fleming, Eds. *Psycholinguistics and the Teaching of Reading.* Newark, Del.: International Reading Association, 1969.

Kintsch, Walter. On Comprehending Stories. Paper presented at the Carnegie Symposium on Cognition, 1976.

Kintsch, Walter, *Representation of Meaning in Memory.* New York, N.Y.: John Wiley and Sons, 1974.

Levin, Harry and Joanna P. Williams, Eds. *Basic Studies in Reading.* New York, N.Y.: Basic Books, 1970.

Lindsay, P.H. and D.A. Norman. *Human Information Processing, An Introduction to Psychology.* New York, N.Y.: Academic Press, 1972.

Morris, Lynn Lyons. The Use of Psychological Bases for Construction of Test Domains in Basic Skills. Paper presented at the annual meeting of the American Educational Research Association, New York, April 1977.

Singer, Harry and Robert B. Ruddell, Eds. *Theoretical Models and Processes of Reading.* 2nd ed. Newark, Del.: International Reading Association, 1976.

Smith, Frank. *Comprehension and Learning.* New York, N.Y.: Holt, Rinehart & Winston, 1975.

Zais, Robert S. *Curriculum Principles and Foundations.* New York, N.Y.: Thomas Y. Crowell Company, 1976.

- *What three prerequisites are identified for effective competency programs in reading?*
- *What are the implications of the authors' call for "Forward to the Basics"?*

FUNCTIONAL READING IN COMPETENCY PROGRAMS

Richard T. Vacca
Jo Anne L. Vacca
Kent State University

In the wake of dissatisfaction with public education has come the impetus for back-to-basics and minimum competencies. Secondary schools are faced with numerous public mandates, not the least of which is to insure that graduates have the minimum reading proficiency needed in adult life.

Some school districts have adopted competency testing for graduation. Some U.S. states (with more likely to follow) have passed laws to insure that students achieve minimum competencies before graduation. Cassidy (1978) used the term "exit competencies." Although there isn't whole-hearted agreement on the nature of an exit competency, at least two questions should be considered: Does the competency help the student search for meaning in written language? Is the competency relevant to a minimal level of success in society?

Remedial programs have become inevitable. One school district in California, reporting on a competency testing program, said, "As a result of the project, more programs for remediation, especially for eleventh and twelfth grade students, were instituted" (Algra, 1978, p. 396). Such programs will not be without their problems. They run some of the risks associated with traditional programs in remedial reading: namely, creating a stigma by setting students apart, and fragmenting learning. Teaching for the test also looms as a potential problem.

Nevertheless, competency programs are here to stay. At least two principles of instruction should guide their development. The first is that reading is never independent of meaning. The second is that reading is never independent of function. In other words, a competency program must empha-

Adapted from *Journal of Reading,* March 1981, *24,* 512-515.

size the functional teaching of reading. For this, certain prerequisites should be kept in mind.

Prerequisite 1:
A working definition of functional reading is essential

The reading curriculum is traditionally organized around *direct* and *functional* instruction. Direct instruction focuses on reading skills arranged according to "scope and sequence" and taught systematically. Emphasis is on developing skills for their own sake, so they can be used eventually in different reading situations. Functional instruction, however, centers around applying skills to real-life tasks. Skills aren't taught or practiced in drill apart from their actual use in a real reading situation.

According to Singer and Donlan (1980), the U.S. Army coined the term functional reading in World War II to refer to a soldier's "ability to understand written instructions for carrying out basic military tasks" (p. 197). Two key words are *carrying out*. Functional instruction means that skills are taught as they are needed and as they are required by the material. Herber (1978) defined it this way:

> Reading is taught functionally (1) when the skills being taught are those which must be used by readers in order to understand the content of an information source...., (2) when those skills are taught *as* the students read the information source, (3) when that information source is assigned in order to teach the content it contains rather than to teach the reading skills it requires (p. 26).

Although Herber applied his concept of functional reading directly to content area instruction, it can be adapted easily to competency programs whose primary purpose is to show students how to read materials that are "out there" in the adult world.

Herber's third point merits particular consideration. Unless the content in functional material is of personal value to students so that they will *want* to read, skill development will be limited. In the long run, functional reading can be defined only in relation to the student's purpose for reading and the requirements of the reading situation. This point leads to a second prerequisite for functional reading in competency programs.

Prerequisite 2:
Material for functional reading should be "real" and timely

Whenever possible, teachers in competency programs should use "real" materials that students will encounter in an adult world. They should bypass artificial materials found in workbooks and kits. In many cases, functional material will reflect the community in which the student lives.

Commercially-produced materials, at best, give students practice in skills. While this is a worthy goal in direct reading instruction, it does not meet the criteria of functional instruction.

Furthermore, functional reading tasks should involve material that is timed to the developmental expectations of students. For example, employment notices in the classified section generally seem irrelevant to seventh graders. However, students who are about to enter the job market will welcome instruction that shows them how to handle an employment notice. When the material is timed to meet students' immediate needs, their motivation is heightened.

Prerequisite 3:
Activities for functional reading should center on meaning

Instructional activities for functional reading should be problem centered and focus on comprehension. Problem solving is a legitimate use of functional reading material. Halliday (1970) noted that cultures having written language tend to formulate and solve problems for which written language is required. Teachers should ask themselves if what they have students do in reading solves any problems that students see as important. When students raise their own questions and make predictions about the material under study, they will approach the reading situation purposefully.

If reading is first and foremost an interplay between the reader and the text, then students must be shown how to use what they already know. The importance of prior knowledge in comprehension has been underscored at the Center for the Study of Reading at the University of Illinois. Anderson and his associates (1977) illustrated just how powerful prior knowledge can be when readers interpret text. As part of an experiment, they asked college level students to read a passage that began, "Rocky slowly got up from the mat, planning his escape" (p. 372). The passage was open to a variety of interpretations. Thus, physical education majors mainly interpreted the "Rocky" passage as being about a wrestling match. On the other hand, criminal justice students mainly felt that the passage was about a prison escape.

Pichert and Anderson (1976) also demonstrated the importance of the reader's perspective. When readers who held the perspective of a house burglar read a story about going through a house, they recalled different information than those readers who approached the story from the perspective of a house buyer.

Creating a hypothetical situation and a role for the student is one way to get "into" reading. Students in these roles find themselves solving problems that force them to use their knowledge and experience. In the following example, Vacca (1981) showed how a high school teacher created a problem-solving situation before assigning a reading selection from an auto mechanics manual.

> Situation: You are the only mechanic on duty when a 4-wheel drive truck with a V-8 engine pulls in for repair. The truck has high mileage, and it appears that the problem may be a worn clutch disc. What tools do you think you will need? What procedures would you follow? Put your answers to these questions under the two columns below.
>
> *Tools needed*   *Procedures*

The activity led to a lively discussion. Students raised additional questions and discussed possible solutions. The teacher kept discussion open-ended and finally suggested that students could verify or alter their solutions by reading the assigned material. Most of them were eager to begin.

A Concluding Comment

These prerequisites for functional reading in competency programs seem so obvious that some might wonder if they were worth mentioning. Unfortunately, the obvious is not necessarily practiced.

Perhaps the back-to-basics movement would seem less reactionary had the call been for "forward-to-basics." Forward-to-basics suggests that reading is never independent of meaning and function, whether in its beginning or advanced stages. In the final analysis, the value of reading lies in using it as a vehicle for understanding, solving problems, and enjoying.

References

Algra, Cecelia. "Meeting the Challenge of a Minimum Reading Graduation Requirement." *Journal of Reading,* vol. 21 (February 1978), pp. 392-97.

Anderson, Richard, et al. "Frameworks for Comprehension." *American Educational Research Journal,* vol. 14 (1977), pp. 367-82.

Cassidy, Jack. "High School Graduation: Exit Competencies." *Journal of Reading,* vol. 21 (February 1978), pp. 398-402.

Halliday, Michael. "Language Structure and Language Function." In *New Horizons in Linguistics,* edited by John Lyons, pp. 140-65. Hammondsworth, Middlesex, England: Penguin Books, 1970.

Herber, Harold. *Teaching Reading in Content Areas.* 2nd ed. Englewood Cliffs, N.J.: Prentice-Hall, 1978.

Pichert, James, and Richard Anderson. *Taking Different Perspectives on a Story.* Technical Report No. 14. Urbana, Ill.: University of Illinois, Urbana-Champaign, Center for the Study of Reading, 1976.

Singer, Harry, and Dan Donlan. *Reading and Learning from Text.* Boston, Mass.: Little, Brown, 1980.

Vacca, Richard. *Content Area Reading.* Boston, Mass.: Little, Brown, 1981.